Soumitra Chatterjee

Soumitra Chatterjee

His Life in Cinema and Beyond

Amitava Nag

SPEAKING TIGER BOOKS LLP
125A, Ground Floor, Shahpur Jat, near Asiad Village,
New Delhi 110049

First published by Speaking Tiger Books in 2023

Copyright © Amitava Nag 2023

ISBN: 978-93-5447-452-1
eISBN: 978-93-5447-419-4

10 9 8 7 6 5 4 3 2 1

Typeset in EB Garamond by SŪRYA, New Delhi
Printed at Shree Maitrey Printech Pvt. Ltd., Noida

All rights reserved.
No part of this publication may be reproduced, transmitted, or stored in a retrieval system, in any form or by any means, electronic, mechanical, photocopying, recording or otherwise, without the prior permission of the publisher.

This book is sold subject to the condition that it shall not, by way of trade or otherwise, be lent, resold, hired out, or otherwise circulated, without the publisher's prior consent, in any form of binding or cover other than that in which it is published.

To all the curious spirits who nurture a bold 'Soumitra' within them.

Contents

Introduction	1
1. Growing Up Wandering	15
2. An Actor Prepares	35
3. A Golden Streak	52
4. Triumph and Turmoil	77
5. Consolidating the Transition	102
6. Beyond Ray	122
7. New Millennium, Newer Challenges	141
8. The King	159
9. Bela Seshe	179
10. A Meandering Quest	188
Acknowledgements	194
Selected List of Top 150 Films	195

List of Plays	201
Selected Works in Doordarshan	203
Bibliography	205
Major Awards	209

Introduction

When my friend and editor, Shantanu Ray Chaudhuri, called me up shortly after Soumitra Chatterjee passed away and asked me to consider writing a biography of sorts, I was truly overwhelmed. I was going through a very difficult time at that point and was trying to cope with an insurmountable grief. More importantly, I never realized, in spite of my close association with Soumitra-babu (as I called him), that his passing away would leave such a void—emotional and creative. I had written the first book on him in English, *Beyond Apu: 20 Favourite Film Roles of Soumitra Chatterjee*, which Shantanu had edited in 2016. Soumitra-babu and I selected the roles on the basis of lengthy interviews with him and my analyses of the films. I worked on the book for over a year since the beginning of 2012, and it was then that I interacted with Soumitra-babu at length and got to know of some of his lonely times.

Till 2018, he was probably busier than most actors in the Bengali film industry. He would dub, act, recite, do theatre, record for CDs of newcomers and also veterans...the list was endless. More often than not, when I would pay him a surprise visit, I would return empty-handed. The security guard at his residence would announce, '*Babu to kaaj-e beriyechhen*'—(Sir has gone out for work). If I called him afterwards, he would always lament, 'Oh, you should have checked before coming all the way. What about the coming Thursday in the evening? Will you be free and will you mind coming over?'

The Thursdays could be any days of the week. He maintained a small diary of sorts and wrote all the engagements he had in it. My formal interviews had found a place in them as well back in 2012 and 2013. He would look up his diary, tell me when he was free and ask me if I could meet him. I guess it was his way of asking someone to pay him a visit—never an authoritative summons but a gentle request.

I am grateful that Soumitra Chatterjee allowed me to visit him regularly in the last couple of years before the COVID pandemic robbed us of one-to-one interactions. It was mostly he who would call me to find out whether I was available in the evenings or not. I seldom missed the opportunity to spend time with him. He was no longer just a film star to me. All his achievements and awards, all his accolades and adorations, were behind us. In those meetings, we discussed poetry since we both persisted with the broken verse; we spoke about love, life, longing and regrets. We spoke about separation and desire, about the time I was looking ahead to and the one he had crossed already in his journey.

We shared information on books. He would show me the ones he was reading. I would tell him about the films I got to see as part of my job as a film critic of world cinema. He was always eager to know new things, eager to relate, argue and criticize. He was curious and I found that to be his strongest trait as he dabbled in different art forms and made his journey in life.

It was when I started translating fifty of his poems into English for *Walking Through the Mist* (incidentally, the first English translation of his poems in book form) that I got a chance to read his poems as a collective, systematically. It was then that I found him to be a loner deep inside. It was that which drove him to try out so many new things in life, to fill the moments of solitude, to tire himself out in work. It was this wish to engage the mind in something apart from his own thoughts that made him seek out friends to visit him in the evenings.

Soumitra Chatterjee in his own room
(Photo Credit: Shreya Goswami)

'I can somehow still manage the mornings and afternoons, but the evenings are difficult,' he once told me post his hospitalization in August 2019. Acting assignments had diminished for him suddenly. He knew a day would come when filmmakers would think twice before offering him a role because of his deteriorating health. I would always remind him at these times, how he had had the longest of stints ever in the annals of Bengali cinema. He would give a wry smile—'But how long, Amitava?'

Soumitra had witnessed enough uncertainties, anxieties and turmoil in his career. He had personal tragedies to deal with as well, some very late in his life. Apart from rare outbursts, he would not discuss them in general. He was tired, mentally and physically. In our shared spaces in the evenings and mornings, he would tell me stories of his early days. I had a lot to question, now informally. There were no recorders that intruded our privacy and made him conscious and reserved.

Speaking to him was always an experience because Soumitra Chatterjee could differentiate memories from nostalgia. That is why he lived in the present and not the lengthening shadows of a glorious past. It is precisely for this reason that he could deliver at least three to four memorable performances in each of the six decades of his career. In the first two decades that number is even higher. He never wanted to become outdated, and he never did. In those discussions that I had with him, he was relaxed. And yet, like a child, he was at times anxious to know a lot of things that happened around us.

We discussed Nobel prizes, I showed him a video of Professor John B. Goodenough who got the award in chemistry in 2019 at the age of ninety-seven. We both laughed at the apparent simplicity of the professor in the interview and agreed that, at the highest level, simplicity is indeed the greatest of all virtues. In his own way, Soumitra-babu did sport his elegant naturalism like a shawl draping his illustrious body of work and accomplishments.

In those last few years of our association, we grew fonder of each other. I guess he felt the same as well, considering how frequently he wanted me to visit his place. And then the lockdown happened in March 2020.

When it started, we were all unsure. How grave was it, the extent, would we survive? Soumitra-babu and I kept in touch over the phone. He was always very logical. He would analyse and explain the precautions we all needed to maintain. A year back, he had written a new play based on Lila Majumder's children's novel *Batas Bari* written in 1974. It was planned to be staged by the children's wing of the theatre group, Mukhomukhi, with whom he had been associated for many years.

Ultimately, on his last birthday, on 19 January 2020, he read out the entire play that he had adapted. It was indeed a unique experience for all of us who listened to that rendition, him enacting all the different characters in his reading and distinguishing each with tonal inflections. In the phone conversations during the lockdown phase, he told me his plans of writing new plays, almost always adaptations. He picked up P.G. Wodehouse, someone whom he had discovered more seriously quite late.

It was only after half the year had gone by in 2020 that I

realized he was becoming extremely frustrated being indoors and restricted. He resumed shooting and was working both on his biopic and also a documentary on him. I was planning to write a book on my conversations with him and was unsure how to go about it. In my first book on him, my aim was to focus on him as an actor who was much more than one who revelled only in the films of Satyajit Ray.

Time and again, in discussions with critics from other parts of the country and abroad, I found him to be referenced as the quintessential Ray actor. And nothing beyond. This irked me a lot, which was why I preferred to keep his Ray appearances to a minimum in *Beyond Apu*. He did buy my point of view then and deep down, I felt that he was probably not very disappointed, if not overtly content, with that book. But for *Murmurs: Silent Steals with Soumitra Chatterjee*, which I began writing in the latter half of 2020, there was no such compulsion. I asked Antara Nanda Mondal of Blue Pencil Publications whether they would be interested in such a book. Antara gave me a free rein, to my relief.

Murmurs was envisaged as a book with a difference. It is not a typical memoir. Most importantly, I never told Soumitra-babu that I was writing the book. I didn't need his interviews as such; there were less facts—rather, my diary notes that I scribbled every time I returned from his place in the last few years or so. In hindsight, I feel guilty that I didn't get a chance to tell him that I was working on *Murmurs*. It took me days to figure out how to write, what all to write. I wished to bring forth a vision of him as an octogenarian who had all the anxieties and frailties of life. I wanted to project him as an ordinary human, not the demigod which the media projected all the time. And yet, reflect upon the finer qualities that set him apart.

And then came 6 October 2020. The day before, I interacted with Poulami-di, his daughter, about the documentary on him. Little did we know then that his admission to a city hospital with moderate fever the very next day would be his last journey out of home. Incidentally, the physical copy of *Walking Through the Mist* was delayed endlessly. He had enquired from me a few times earlier about the possible date of a paperback edition. (It was already published in Kindle format earlier in 2020.) He had approved my translation of his poems already but wished to feel it in his hands. Finally, the book reached his residence the day he left for hospital.

Looking back, I now think his month-and-a-half hospitalization changed perspectives for me. His condition ebbed and flowed; the Durga Puja came and went in a whiff, the pandemic made things worse, my own mental and physical health and that of the family went through ups and downs. It was then that my writing found its course. It flowed, with emotion, with reflections, it was emotionally extremely draining.

When Shantanu asked me to write on him, I was too full of emotions to think hard and decide. I agreed because, though Soumitra-babu never gave me that duty, yet, deep inside me, I felt I had a responsibility towards him, and I needed some solace for my beaten soul. Shantanu and I agreed that it would be a biography of sorts, not veering on gossip but relying on his journey from his childhood till the end. By reading all the stories that were written on him and some that he chose to tell me personally, I knew a lot about him. Or so I thought.

It was when I started reading up on him and the essays that he wrote that I realized how much more there was to know. It was for the first time that I discerned how I wanted to speak to him again, ask him the questions that I had never cared to ask before. That left me feeling vacant and hollow.

On one hand, Soumitra Chatterjee had a poetic mind, always seeking to unravel the mysteries of nature, to deep-dive into the unknown crevices of the mind. Poetry gave him shelter, it gave him a mask to hide behind and write the words he intended to. Yet, poetry was where he was most transparent, as if like a reflector that expressed the pain and celebrated the joys of him as a human being. Alongside, as an editor of *Ekshan*, he played the role of an archivist whereby he and his co-editor, Nirmalya Acharya, decided to have a section on memoirs of women writers of the nineteenth century. These two roles—that of a nibbler, a dreamer, and the other of a preserver—complement his mind, hungry for creative pursuits.

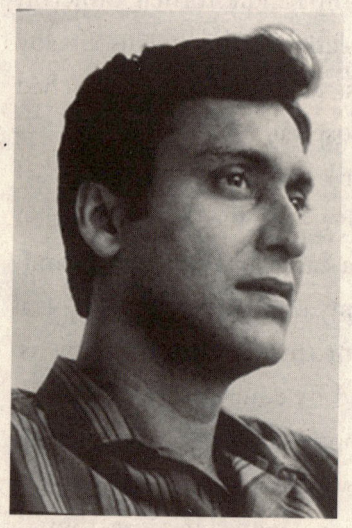

A young and strikingly handsome Soumitra Chatterjee
(Photo Credit: Sukumar Roy)

It is to be noted that since the capital of the British Raj shifted to Delhi in 1911, followed by the Great Bengal Famine of 1943 and the partition of Bengal in 1947, Calcutta was already falling behind other Indian metropolitan cities. Even some of the non-metros in north and south India had started developing at an awe-inspiring pace. However, one area where Calcutta was still distinguished was in the arts—literature and cinema being the two most prominent.

From the likes of Rabindranath Tagore, Saratchandra Chatterjee, Bankimchandra Chatterjee and Michael Madhusudan Dutt, Calcutta had a riches of writers, poets and novelists which no other part of the country could produce. Alongside, there were social reformists, like Raja Rammohan Roy and Ishwar Chandra Vidyasagar, philosophers and preachers of Hindu religion in Swami Vivekananda and Ramakrishna Paramahansa, and thousands of gallant freedom fighters led by selfless leaders like Rashbehari Bose, Arabinda Ghosh and—the most revered of all—Netaji Subhas Chandra Bose.

Calcutta, till the first three decades of the twentieth century, was the cradle of culture, education and enlightenment. This proud history is one of the reasons that made Soumitra loyal to his mother tongue and native land. He did move out of his ancestral home and settled in urban Calcutta for his higher education and career, but he didn't wish to change shores in pursuit of bigger fame and more money. He eventually achieved international recognition even by staying in his quaint home in South Calcutta.

A human being is defined by the options he faces and the choices he can make. Constraints at one time turn to opportunities at another. If someone traces the trajectory of Soumitra's journey through the first two decades of his acting career, from 1959 till 1980, one will be startled by his varied activities. He had a dream start, almost like a Sachin Tendulkar in cinema—young and successful. And like Tendulkar, Soumitra also batted very, very long, changing his stance as required. From 1959 till 1965, he had the opportunity of acting in the films of all great contemporary directors of Bengal, apart from Ritwik Ghatak. Most other actors, including Uttam Kumar, the biggest star of Bengali cinema at that time, could not boast of such a feat. Only Anil Chatterjee had that fortune but he was never a match for Soumitra in terms of stardom or the offers that came Soumitra's way.

In many personal conversations as well as in interviews, Soumitra iterated time and again without any doubt or hesitation that he was lucky to get some of the best roles in Bengali cinema in the 1960s. It was the humility of the actor. He deserved all of them. He was every bit what Uttam Kumar was not. He was a people's representative and yet could be uniquely peerless due to his markedly handsome looks, which wasn't and isn't that common in this part of the land. He is, if I may say, like Charlie Chaplin whose tramp is universal and yet poignantly matchless and exclusive.

Riding such a high, Soumitra never lost track of his literary lineage—he recited poetry in functions, wrote poems in abundance and edited the magazine *Ekshan*. He was indeed a polymath, a man who wore many hats; most importantly, in the shallow Bengali alley of thinkers, he was a doer, like his mentor, Satyajit Ray.

A keen observer of the changing times, he changed his looks to suit the new age. His wardrobe changed, so did his hairstyle. His profiles became outgoing in cinema, as internally he was moving to his theatrical roots silently in the 1970s. He started to act in Bengali commercial theatre with a professional zeal which had been missing for a while. Most of his plays were box office successes though he couldn't evade the final shutdown of the commercial stage. But that didn't stop Soumitra from changing gears and adapting to the basic premises of group theatre and bringing in his aesthetic to it. All of these—his poems, his theatre, his elocution—kept him grounded in Bengali culture. He understood that settling in Mumbai would rob him of these pleasures.

In this book, I trace his initial years of searching for identities and then the final decades of consolidation. He remained a phenomenon till his very end, though the term has lost its relevance, having been used for lesser successes. He was on the Bengali psyche almost like a drape shrouding our own existence. That is why when he was fighting for his life in the hospital, the Bengali diaspora worldwide felt so devastated. He was the last of the magicians, descending from Tagore, to Ray and then him. Amartya Sen is the other pride but his relevance in the minds of the commoner is dubious at best.

All throughout his grim battle against COVID, I was bombarded by friends and strangers on whether I knew any inside information about his health. People started spreading rumours, they wailed and prayed. I could understand it was their uncontrollable passion, their unharnessed emotion that was doing the talking. Everyone feared how they would cope with grief. So did I.

When I started writing this book, I played his entire journey in my mind several times. So many documentations are available today. Much wrong information, mostly personal anecdotes. I have tried to shy away from private stories unless they highlight any of the choices he exercised based on the options he had at hand. To me, intimate stories lack efficacy in a biography. He never believed in biographies—auto or otherwise. But he did write, direct and act *Tritiyo Onko, Otoeb*, which was autobiographical. And then he agreed to be part of a biopic and a documentary on him as well.

I am not sure what his reaction would have been if he heard I was writing this book. In my defence, this one is a far cry from the ones he despised, I am sure. I wanted to find the missing links in his creative pursuits, connecting the dots in front of me. I so wished he would check them and approve this book the way he did so many others before this one. But probably not. Let my own findings unravel the mystery behind his creative genius.

Amitava Nag with Soumitra Chatterjee
(Photo Credit: Amitava Nag)

If my readers find meaning in my correlations as well, I will be more than happy. For once, let Soumitra Chatterjee sit back and watch his life unravel before him.

ONE

Growing Up Wandering

Kusthia was a part of Nadia district under the Bengal Province of British India. It was in Shilaidaha of Kusthia that the Tagores had a country house. Nobel poet laureate Rabindranath Tagore spent a significant creative part of his life in the country house at Shilaidaha at the turn of the last century from 1890 onwards. It was during this phase that he would write his acclaimed poetry collections, *Sonar Tari* and *Katha o Kahini*, and start translating *Gitanjali* into English. Kusthia was also the ancestral land of mystic poet, Baul saint and philosopher, Lalon Fakir, who inspired several poets including Rabindranath.

During British rule, Kusthia was only a municipality under the Nadia district. It had a river port and a railway connection to Calcutta, thanks to its growing indigo and jute plantations. It was during the partition of India in 1947 that Kusthia, along with two other subdivisions of Nadia district, were detached from India and made part of a new, larger Kusthia district of what was then East Pakistan.

Kayagram, a village in Kusthia, is encircled by the Garui river. Ramkinkar Chatterjee, whose ancestral home was in the Nalua village of Jessore district, married and settled in the Kalna town of Burdwan. Ramkinkar's son Gourmohan also migrated like his father, married and built a residence in Kayagram. Gourmohan's son, Ramsundar, established their roots more firmly. He built 'Basanta Villa' where the Chatterjees resided for a few generations. Ramsundar was one of the wealthy 'jotdars' under the zamindari of Debendranath Tagore who ran the estate from Shilaidaha. An able administrator, Ramsundar earned the appreciation of Debendranath for his administrative skills and ability to manage both the Hindu and Muslim subjects of the estate.

Ramsundar had five grandsons and two granddaughters. The eldest granddaughter Saratsashi, widowed with a young son at an early age, stayed with the family at Kayagram itself. Saratsashi's son, Jatindranath Mukherjee, better known as Bagha Jatin, was one of Bengal's earliest revolutionary freedom fighters who died fighting the British. Jatindranath's close aide was his uncle, Saratsashi's youngest brother, Lalit Kumar.

After graduating in law, Lalit Kumar started practising professionally from Krishnanagar from 1903. He was also the estate lawyer of the Tagores and other zamindars in nearby places. Since 1904-05, Lalit Kumar was also involved in the freedom struggle of India and inspired his nephew Jatindranath to join the revolution. In 1910, both Lalit Kumar and Jatindranath were arrested in connection with the Howrah-Sibpur conspiracy case, popularly known as the Howrah Gang Case. Lalit Kumar was shifted to a solitary cell in the Presidency Jail and was discharged after six months due to lack of evidence.

Though constantly in touch with revolutionary leaders, Lalit Kumar gradually got more involved in his profession and eventually became an advocate in the Calcutta High Court, staying in Krishnanagar. In Krishnanagar, he was the president of the Bar Association of lawyers. A distinguished Bengali of the town, Lalit Kumar held several important positions in multiple banks and was part of the managing committees of several schools. A patron of Bengali culture, it was Lalit Kumar's enterprise that led to a historic Bengali-language literary convention organized at the Krishnanagar palace and presided over by the litterateur Pramatha Chaudhuri.

Lalit Kumar's wife was Sudhamoyi Debi, the granddaughter of legendary Sanskrit pandit, Madan Mohan Tarkalankar. The Bengali language is forever indebted to Tarkalankar for devising books that are revered as the first few to teach the language. As important as his compatriot Ishwar Chandra Vidyasagar's *Barnaparichay*, Tarkalankar's three-volume *Sishu Siksha* actually predates *Barnaparichay*. Along with Vidyasagar, Tarkalankar was instrumental in women's education as well as the Hindu remarriage movement of young widows.

Lalit Kumar and Sudhamoyi had two sons—Mohit Kumar and Suhrid Kumar—and a daughter, Tara. Tara was married to Ramaprasad Mukherjee, son of Sir Ashutosh Mukherjee, popularly known as 'Banglar Bagh' aka 'Bengal Tiger'. Mohit Kumar, married to Ashalata Devi, had three sons—Sambit, Soumitra and Abhijit—and a daughter, Anuradha.

Soumitra had fond memories of his grandfather Lalit Kumar

and an impish sense of pride in his lineage with Bagha Jatin. His penchant for the Bengali language, his rootedness to the Bengali culture and the spirit of his adventurous mind probably owed itself to his enlightened family legacy.

A rare old photo of Soumitra's family. Here, he is standing second from left, as a young boy, in the second row.
(Photo Credit: Poulami Chatterjee)

***

It was an exceptionally cold full-moon Saturday night when Soumitra was born on the nineteenth day of January in the year 1935. Ashalata Devi gave birth to her second child at her maternal house in Calcutta as was the custom of the time. A fervent reader of books, Ashalata was especially fond of Michael Madhusudhan Dutt's remarkable epic poem, *Mehnadbadh Kabya* on the demise of the tragic hero Meghnad at the hands of Lakshman in the classic epic Ramayana. More than Meghnad, it was Lakshman, referred to as Soumitri Keshari (son of Sumitra), who attracted Ashalata's imagination and adoration. Drawing inspiration from the classic, Ashalata named her son Soumitra.

Growing up in Krishnanagar had a direct influence on Soumitra's mind. Krishnanagar was a culturally enriched town, with literary stalwarts including Dwijendra Lal Roy hailing from it. There was a traditional wit and humour of the place that dated back to the court culture of the Raja Krishna Chandra after whom the city was named. Though the numerous comic stories of Gopal Bhaad, the court jester of Raja Krishna Chandra, seem fictitious, there is no doubt that life had been joyful, simple and laced with humour that enveloped the citizens of Krishnanagar. Soumitra imbibed this culture of wit in his persona and life, which helped him remain grounded and prevented him from being overwhelmed by the vicissitudes of life.

An extremely naughty and restless child, Soumitra was close to his elder brother Sambit, who was only a year and a half older than him. It was Sambit who used to affectionately call his baby brother 'ulu, mulu, pulu' from where Soumitra's pet name 'Pulu' came to stay. From an early age though, books attracted Soumitra and elders found that a ploy to keep him away from mischievous activities. Both father Mohit Kumar and grandfather Lalit Kumar loved acting and the former used to act in amateur theatre groups that existed at that time. Being

Soumitra (extreme left) with his elder brother Sambit and parents
(Photo Credit: Poulami Chatterjee)

the city of the great author and playwright Dwijendra Lal Roy, there were several regular theatre productions at Krishnanagar.

At the same time, recitation was a vocation quite in vogue at 'Sudha Nilay', the residence of the Chatterjees. Even during his own student days, Mohit Kumar used to participate in recitation competitions organized by the University of Calcutta and won several prizes. Lalit Kumar, who was also fond of recitation, used to inspire his grandchildren to recite Bengali as well as English poems. It was this environment at home that created a natural liking for poetry in Soumitra.

There was another intrinsic reason. The house hosted a big collection of books which both Mohit Kumar and Ashalata had received as prizes from their respective schools. The books were varied, on literature and also a few on recitation. Ashalata was not proficient in singing. Instead, she used to read out a lot of poems to her children to put them to sleep, which mostly included the ones from Rabindranath Tagore's *Sishu* and *Sishu Bholanath*.

One particular incident remained etched in Soumitra's young mind. Suffering from fever, Soumitra didn't go to school that day—8 August 1941. It was midday when Sambit returned early from school. Ashalata asked her eldest son who explained the reason for the unplanned holiday—Rabindranath Tagore had passed away the day before! Soumitra recollected in vivid detail how his mother broke into instant tears hearing the news, slowly sitting on the ground holding the railings of their veranda. Much later he could fathom the extent of Rabindranath's impact on the Bengali mind such that a common housewife would also be so immensely moved by the death of a poet.

In Calcutta, the family would visit primarily two relatives, both eminent in their own ways. The father-in-law of Soumitra's paternal aunt was Sir Ashutosh Mukherjee, educationist, jurist and barrister and also father of politician Shyamaprasad Mukherjee. Though the majority of books were in English, Soumitra was eternally drawn to the huge, princely library at Mukherjee's house primarily because there was a handy collection of foreign books with excellent pictures and texts.

The other house the Chatterjees visited in Calcutta belonged to author Sourindra Mohan Mukhopadhyay, Ashalata's uncle-in-law. This house also had a library, albeit a much smaller one but what attracted young Soumitra to it was the spread of Bengali books which he could savour very easily. There was another attraction—to listen to his aunt, Ashalata's cousin, Suchitra's, vocal renditions first-hand. Suchitra went on to become one of the finest exponents of Rabindra Sangeet in a few years' time.

Addiction to books however didn't bind him indoors all the time. He was an avid sportsperson throughout his active life, preferring athletics, and remained a constant winner of competitions throughout his school days. A natural sportsperson, Soumitra was a deft hockey player and played in a second division club in Calcutta much later while studying in college.

Apart from books and sports, the other attraction which Soumitra couldn't resist was to visit Chitramandir, the lone cinema hall in Krishnanagar at that time. Even at a young age, he would bunk school and book tickets priced at 2 paise to sit on wooden benches to gorge on films—from Charlie Chaplin to the New Theatre ones.

***

Soumitra was admitted to Class I in the CMS, St John's High School. Run by Christian missionaries, the school was one of the oldest and quite famous in Krishnanagar at that time.

There was a nice, quaint Protestant church associated with the school which was linked to the Church of England. The bigger church in Krishnanagar was however a Catholic one run by Italian missionaries. Krishnanagar was a peaceful secular place at that time where people from different religions mingled and mixed freely with each other.

At a later time, Soumitra would recollect the celebration they took part in during Christmas, participating in stick fighting during Moharram, Muslim coachmen dancing to the tune of 'dhaak' in Jagaddhatri Puja and Christians visiting families to seek blessings on *Bijoya Dashami* at the end of Durga Puja. This sense of religious harmony had a bearing on the young minds who grew up at that time. Soumitra was deeply influenced as well, and it helped him tide over political developments that attempted to tear down the fabric of peace that prevailed earlier.

From Classes I till V, Miss McArthur, a British lady, was the principal. She was a very affectionate person by heart though she had a stern disciplinarian exterior in order to manage a co-educational school. She was very fond of Soumitra and believed that he could do no wrong. Soumitra recalls, 'Miss McArthur had to face a very embarrassing situation once that involved me. My father had visited the school to get a friend's son admitted and principal madam was all in praise of me. She then escorted my father to my class just to show how diligent I was as a student. I was in Class I at that time and extremely naughty. At that particular time, I had been punished and made to stand on the bench! Seeing me there, Miss McArthur was shocked and embarrassed more than my father and she kept on repeating that there must have been a mistake somewhere. There was, in not knowing what a chimp I was actually.'*

Madhusudan Bhattacharya, who lived in Nagendranagar area in Krishnanagar, was a friend of Soumitra since Class I. Malay Modak was another friend who completed the holy trinity in school. Soumitra's house had a wonderful cultural environment. Even at that young age, his friends could feel an unmistakable attraction to it. But the trio had many adventures as well. On the other side of the Jalangi river, they would occasionally raid the gram fields and were frequently chased by security guards.

Madhusudan recalls how strong their bond was as friends. 'The three of us had a hidden bank next to Malay's house, in a small field, away from prying eyes. A hole was dug in the ground and it was covered with bricks. Hiding from everyone, money was collected and deposited in that 'bank'. Then, if necessary, we withdrew from our own bank and had food and drinks of our choice. One day, we found that the bricks were removed and our bank was empty.'

It was in their own home that Soumitra, along with his siblings and cousins, would stage plays based on those available for children. They would prepare the stage themselves with the home furniture and would use bedsheets for curtains and Ashalata's saris for creating the backstage wings. Needless to say, the production got approval and appreciation from Lalit Kumar and Mohit while Ashalata helped the children in their

---

* Soumitra Chatterjee, *Gadya Sangraha*, Volume 1, Dey's Publishing, 2016, p. 302—translated by the author.

makeup with tin foils. Neighbours, servants and friends formed the encouraging audience.

It was in this home production that Soumitra acted in a Rabindranath play for the first time, *Mukut* (*The Crown*). Acting was alluring for Soumitra at that time. He remembered how once, when a client of his grandfather entrusted him to keep an eye on a suitcase with valuables, he took it to the neighbours and feigned that he was fleeing to Bombay with all the money. So convincing was his acting that the neighbours fell for the prank and it was only when they threatened to hand him over to his parents did he break into laughter—to everyone's relief.

However, Soumitra's official public performance happened at the end of Class V. The annual examination was over and the prize distribution ceremony was about to take place. Around these events, excitement kept rising among the young ones. At that time, 1944-45, entertainment in mofussil towns like Krishnanagar was defined by cinema in Chitramandir cinema hall, theatre in temporary, makeshift stages, music conferences and literary festivals. However, the little ones didn't have access to any of these. As a result, school programmes were the only source of enjoyment for them. That year, in the annual school programme, a theatre production became the main attraction.

Based on a folklore, the play *The Sleeping Princess* was directed by the principal, Miss McArthur, herself. Being a co-education school, there was no problem with getting female characters. Soumitra was an automatic choice for a role since he used to recite English poems all through the previous years. Reba Dutt played the role of the princess and Kumkum Roy, the role of queen. Among the male characters, Akram was cast in the role of prince, while Soumitra played the king. A relative of Miss McArthur, who was associated with the British stage theatre, visited her at the time of rehearsals. He helped the young group with their acting.

In later reminiscences, Soumitra recounted how in one scene of begging, their tutor asked them to feel the emotion that someone would feel when begging for a handful of rice. It was a rudimentary acting technique to base emotions of one activity in depicting some other, a lesson that Soumitra never forgot even when he took up acting professionally.

The performance happened in front of a packed audience in the school auditorium and it was adored by all who watched it. Madhusudan recounts, 'The play was so good that even after seven decades, the memory of the play is still fresh in my mind. Soumitra, the little king of *The Sleeping Princess*, my schoolmate at the time, the doyen and preserver of Bengali culture, was still in the womb of future. Miss McArthur was his first director. And I, a fascinated viewer of his first stage performance.'

In those days, distinguished members of the audience used to award medals to celebrate performances that they liked. Soumitra bagged a couple of medals for his acting. This hunger for success and craving for appreciation were ingrained in Soumitra in childhood and lured him to acting more and more.

Acting worked as a shield to escape from the mundane realities of life. Soumitra was allergic to institutional education though he was a passionate reader. The accolades in acting helped him with his self-belief. More importantly, there were doubts about his looks, hailing as he did from a family of handsome boys and beautiful girls. Putting up a mask and camouflaging as someone else also helped boost Soumitra's confidence.

There was another reason for fostering an inferiority complex in his mind. At the age of eight, Soumitra once suffered from the deadly typhoid disease. He was down with fever for sixty-three days. Being bedridden

Soumitra with his elder brother Sambit
(Photo Credit: Poulami Chatterjee)

for three months made him forget how to walk. At that age, Soumitra had to learn to walk all over again. He was into physical activities and played different outdoor sports, yet his calf muscles remained underdeveloped which added to his perennial doubts about his physical strength. This scepticism about his own abilities and value drove Soumitra well into his later years and he strived to find meaning in his work, resulting in a curious search for the unknown. It is this penchant to unravel and discover which led him to explore new avenues, from writing to painting.

It was at nearly the same time that the great Bengal famine devastated the equilibrium of Bengal in 1942-43. A manmade disaster of epic proportions, it was another ploy, after the unsuccessful attempt to partition Bengal in 1905, to destabilize the Indian economy and weaken Bengal's political supremacy. Food was heavily rationed and new terms came into the Bengali vocabulary including 'Agoon Daam', 'Chaal Aakra' and 'Maggi Gondar Bajar', which referred to the sky-high price of everyday commodities. Soumitra and Sambit had to stand in queues for the daily share of rice and daal and would return empty-handed a few times when the supplies got over before their turn had come.

After seven decades, Soumitra vividly remembered the shattering sights of corpses on the streets and the heart-wrenching cry for food. 'One who has ever heard that wail will never be able to forget it. It also created a sense of value, not to waste, never to squander what you have received,' he would comment in private discussions time and again.

There was another incident etched in Soumitra's young mind forever. There was an unknown, decrepit man who took shelter in the neighbour's veranda. He was a mere skeleton covered with skin, fragile, weak. Soumitra would keep aside a part of his daily food ration and serve it to the man who could neither speak nor get up due to weeks of malnutrition, or maybe worse. One night, Soumitra couldn't steal out of his house; the next morning, the man was found dead. It was Soumitra's first encounter with death.

After thirty years, when his mentor Satyajit Ray asked him to portray the role of the priest Gangacharan in *Ashani Sanket* with the backdrop of famine, Soumitra approached the role with authenticity and painful realism.

***

Indian independence has a strange history involving a few parts of Bengal including Krishnanagar and some of the other areas of Nadia. Sir Cyril Radcliffe, who was entrusted with drawing borders for the new nations of India and Pakistan, wrongly awarded a chunk of Nadia to East Pakistan, as latter-day Bangladesh was known at the time. For three days, from 14 to 16 August, these areas were considered to be parts of Pakistan with Pakistan's flags flying over them. A huge crisis ensued, petitions were submitted against the mistake and finally, on 17 August, there was an official announcement by the Radcliffe Commission that only three Muslim-majority subdivisions of Nadia (Meherpur, Chuadanga and Kusthia) and portions of three other districts (Malda, Dinajpur and Jalpaiguri) would go to East Pakistan. The rest, including Krishnanagar, would remain with India although the Chatterjees' ancestral home in Kayagram became a foreign country.

'For three days, we became citizens of Pakistan,' Soumitra would chuckle, 'but I think these twists and turns in history and the different experiences made me ambivalent to larger differences that many thrived on. For that matter, the whole debate between 'ghati' [meaning the people of West Bengal] and 'bangal' [meaning the people of East Bengal] seemed superfluous to me from an early age. I was an admirer of both Mohun Bagan and East Bengal; since then, I just found it difficult to take sides.'

Growing up, Soumitra was a wanderer. A free bird, he would roam around the streets, befriending young boys of his age. Boisterous and quick to rise to provocations, he was the de facto leader of the gang in school. It was probably more out of his compulsion to be accepted the way he was, rather than be second fiddle to Sambit who was an academically brilliant student.

From 1945 onwards, the family shifted base continuously and Soumitra had to change schools regularly. It affected his studies but at the same time, it exposed him to people of different streams of life as well as landscapes of different hues and colour. Mohit Kumar Chatterjee was practising law in the Calcutta High Court till then and in 1945, he took a job in the Civil Supply Department. The family changed base and shifted to Barasat near Calcutta. In Barasat, Soumitra was admitted to the Barasat Government High School. Mohit Kumar's transferable job ensured that the family moved to Howrah a year later. Soumitra was forced to change school yet again, this time the Howrah Zilla School.

It was in Barasat that Soumitra found himself in the midst of an incident he would recall proudly later on. At that time, a group of INA soldiers who were prisoners of the British government were passing through the Barasat station. There was a huge interest in seeing the brave soldiers who were ready to lay down their lives under the able guidance of Netaji Subhas Chandra Bose. A Sikh soldier asked Soumitra to bring drinking water for him, and he willingly did so. The Sikh asked him, 'Which race are you, young boy?' to which young Soumitra beamingly replied, 'Indian.' Needless to say, the Sikh soldier was overwhelmed and carried Soumitra on his shoulder.

'Since childhood, we grew up in a very patriotic environment. Not only were we aware of many stories of Bagha Jatin, his bravery and the resistance he put up against the British but we also heard a few of my grandfather as well. Even my father was imprisoned by the British for his activities. We also heard that once, Netaji came to Krishnanagar for a meeting. He visited my grandfather and had tea at our house. The porcelain tea set in which he was served tea was never used in our house again. He gave an autograph to my father and in our childhood, I remember the goosebumps we would feel looking at Netaji's signature every single time.'

However, while in Howrah in 1946, Soumitra experienced the bitter side of India's freedom struggle—the Hindu-Muslim riots that rocked the nation and particularly Bengal. In front of his eyes, Soumitra witnessed how years-long relations turned vicious in the name of religion. Memories of communal harmony in Krishnanagar only a few years before seemed almost unreal. It was here that Soumitra witnessed murder for the first time.

There was a Muslim shop in the locality. When the riot broke out, everyone fled apart from one hapless employee hiding in it. Soon, he was hounded out of his hideaway and chased by an angry mob. The man started running with a dagger in his back and a flock of men rushing after him, baying for his blood. The man dropped dead soon but the memory of him scampering for life, blood oozing from his back, trying to flee, remained vivid in Soumitra's mind. Running away had been a constant refrain for Soumitra—from life, from death as well.

In this time of erosion—of values and virtues—at the advent of puberty, Soumitra was looking for lost grounds. Poems, not only the ones recited by his parents but the ones written by him, started to play an important part. It was this that would provide him with the necessary shelter and also prepare him for the future. Every time, for the next seven decades of his life.

Two other things worked with clockwork precision in Soumitra's life right from those early days. The first was his interest, efficacy and capacity to pursue several sports activities. He was a natural athlete but also took up boxing, cycling and other forms of exercise, apart from hockey which he pursued longer than the others, till his late college years. The other interest was acting.

Howrah is the twin city of Calcutta. Even during that time, it was a thriving city due to this physical proximity. It was in Howrah that there were several theatre groups, many more than in Krishnanagar, and definitely more professionally oriented with commendable stage productions. Soumitra would soon influence friends to form a theatre group themselves; the hunger for acting and to hide behind the mask of others and gain accolades fanned his decision. Becoming an actor was still not a professional choice. It was rather a vocation that he enjoyed with vigour and purpose.

Manmatha Mukherjee was a small-time hero in films who used to stay in the same locality as Soumitra. Manmatha was a theatre actor as well. Watching an actor of cinema and theatre from close quarters inspired Soumitra immensely. Acting was slowly becoming an addiction that he couldn't shrug off. *Maharaja Nandakumar* and *Siraj ud-Daulah* were two plays that Soumitra's theatre group would stage eventually, after watching Manmatha's theatre group perform both. Soumitra would follow Manmatha's histrionics at that young age with a fair amount of success. Yet, he was unwilling to accompany friends to watch commercial Bengali theatre in Calcutta, fearing he would be heavily influenced by the prevalent acting styles of professional theatre.

After staying in Howrah for three years, the family migrated again, now to Darjeeling. Darjeeling was culturally an antithesis of Krishnanagar, Barasat and Howrah. Theatre and acting were out of range in that milieu. But the lure of nature became deeply ingrained in Soumitra's mind. The magnificence of the Himalayas engrossed him completely. His father would tour different areas in the mountains; Soumitra and his younger brother Abhijit would accompany him everywhere. The mental nourishment from nature was so complete that Soumitra started nurturing a desire to be a globetrotter.

The imageries of the mountains were vivid in Soumitra's memories, his perception of beauty was defined by that one year in the Himalayas. Decades later when he started painting, it was the mountains and the jungles that came back as a recurrent theme in his landscapes.

The stint in Darjeeling was for a year and the family moved back to Krishnanagar again for a few months due to Lalit Kumar's ill health. Soumitra was admitted to the Krishnanagar Collegiate School and his passion and penchant for theatre returned and resurfaced. It was at this time that he played Karna in *Naranarayan*. Bengal's second governor, Kailash Nath Katju, was among the guests in the audience and he presented Soumitra with a medal for his performance. With the death of Lalit Kumar, the family moved to Howrah again.

Howrah had an important impact in Soumitra's life. It fostered him and prepared him for the big leap that was to come. It was in Howrah that he befriended artist Rabin Mondal who was six years senior to him. Soumitra would shadow Rabin multiple times in the latter's sketching expeditions and, unconsciously enough, picked up the habit of drawing himself. On the other side of the mental spectrum, it was during this period that Soumitra was friends with a number of bus and taxi drivers of Howrah. He would ride with them in the public buses and roam around the city, watch people, soak in life. A hungry, curious mind defines the ageless spontaneity of Soumitra Chatterjee.

A decade later, while enacting Narsingh in *Abhijan*, he gave Satyajit Ray valuable inputs about certain traits, patterns in dialogue delivery and physical mannerisms. Ray included them readily. It was in Howrah that Soumitra fell in love with Deepa when he was in Class X. Deepa was a friend of his sister, Anuradha, a student of Howrah Girls' School. Romantic liaisons were difficult in those days. It was no different for Soumitra. Deepa was an avid reader and a sportsperson herself. She would later, after their marriage, become a state-level badminton champion in West Bengal.

In 1951, Soumitra passed matriculation from the Howrah Zilla School and wandered again, now to Calcutta. Calcutta was an El Dorado for many, a harbinger of spring and hope. Soumitra eventually made Calcutta his home, his food for sustenance, his anchor to express art in life. Calcutta broadened his vision. It was to his credit that he was never oblivious of the varied impacts of his wondrous childhood days. The success of Soumitra Chatterjee as a creative human being lies in how he valued his rootlessness even when he deepened his roots in the big city.

TWO

An Actor Prepares

For Soumitra, Calcutta was not a distant mirage. Krishnanagar is only a hundred kilometres away from Calcutta, while Barasat and Howrah are even closer. Howrah being a twin city had been quite similar in scope, only the scale and magnitude differed. Having his maternal grandfather's house in Mirzapur Street in Calcutta meant that the family frequented British India's erstwhile capital quite often.

After completing his matriculation, Soumitra got admitted to City College at Amherst Street in the intermediate science stream. Science was the automatic option for most Bengali middle-class families; even now, things haven't changed psychologically. Mathematics had been a constant threat to Soumitra even in lower classes. He was rather fond of geography, securing 80 per cent marks in the subject in matriculation. His love for geography was probably due to his wanderer, globetrotting dreams. After passing out of intermediate science,

Soumitra enrolled himself in an honours course in Bengali literature in the same college.

For every young adult even today, college is the first flight to uninhibited freedom. The free wings to embrace life to the fullest and enrich it for a lifetime. It was no different for Soumitra. While studying intermediate science in City College, Soumitra had the rare opportunity to attend the classes of Narayan Ganguly, noted author, essayist and creator of the popular young-adult character 'Teni-da' in Bengali literature. Ganguly had a very charismatic personality, handsome looks and a gift of oration that mesmerized the students, including Soumitra.

Soumitra recollected, 'Narayan-babu had an extremely captivating delivery. Those who were fortunate enough to attend his classes were bound to develop a love for literature. My decision to study Bengali at the undergraduate level was based partially on the love of language that germinated from the lectures of Professor Ganguly in particular. The first piece that he taught us was 'Bankimchandra' written by Rabindranath. In that article, Rabindranath narrated an incident when, in a felicitation programme, Bankimchandra garlanded Rabindranath with his own floral wreath, welcoming the young writer as the one who had come to stay.

'Narayan-babu read the narration in a very emotive way and then rendered a touching description: „The crescent moon of the fading night garlanded the rising sun of a young dawn." I will never forget such a description. Narayan-babu loved me a lot. I played Raja Rammohan Roy for the first time in the play *Rammohan* written by him. I remember he showered me with praises—"One day, you will become a very powerful actor. Then I will write your biography." When we graduated from City College in 1955, Sir also left college and joined the Post-Graduate College of Arts in the Bengali department.'

In City College, Soumitra found himself in the midst of friends who were vibrant and curious in their own ways. That included latter-day academician-cum-essayist Sudhir Chakraborty, poets Shakti Chatterjee, Sunil Ganguly, Amitava Dasgupta, writer Tarapada Ray and editor Nirmalya Acharya. But the most influential of all was Gourmohan Mukherjee who was a few classes senior to Soumitra. Mukherjee had a big fan base in college and Soumitra enrolled himself into this admiration club.

There were reasons behind Mukherjee's prolific popularity. It was he who first made them understand how and why structured reading habits were required for a systematic understanding of any subject matter. Himself an erudite scholar, Mukherjee was an exceptional student and encouraged his junior friends to spend time in libraries and open themselves up to diverse genres of writing. Soumitra started getting interested in literary reviews, critiques, history, aesthetics and perspectives, thanks to their beloved 'Gour-da'. It was he who instilled a discipline in the writer in Soumitra by forcing him to write daily. 'Gour-da would always say, "Not a day without a line"; a habit that helped me continue writing continuously for so many years,' Soumitra reminisced later.

The group used to meet at the Coffee House at College Street. Anyone familiar with the city of Calcutta and who has frequented the Coffee House at College Street will swear by its infectious fervour. The jam-packed eating joint on a busy street close to several colleges and institutes in central Calcutta thrives on discussions, almost always animated, between groups that are diverse and different. The high point of the Coffee House remains in its ability to provide a level playing field for both established poets and wannabes. It was here that Soumitra became close to Shakti Chatterjee and Sunil Ganguly, who were then struggling with a newly founded magazine, *Krittibas*.

With his poet friends Shakti Chattopadhyay and Amitava Dasgupta
(Photo Credit: Meenakshi Chattopadhyay)

Founded in 1953, *Krittibas* was an influential literary magazine right from its inception. These influences and confluences enriched Soumitra significantly. It was his friendship with these avant-garde poets that opened his vision to a modern diction of Bengali poetry, which was then desperate to break away from the influences of Tagore. Discussions and debates mostly revolved around literature, cinema and theatre. At a later time, Soumitra recalled how each individual of the group would egg the other on to write regularly. It was at the Coffee House that Soumitra and his classmate Nirmalya would dream of making a serious literary magazine themselves, and *Ekshan* was born, years later, in 1961.

This initiation to the Coffee House, interacting with friends, the ambience that was friendly yet sublimely competitive, was instrumental in shaping Soumitra's creative mind. It may be ascertained with a fair amount of surety that this cultural environment kept Soumitra grounded throughout his life. Even as a star, naturalism never deserted him. Soumitra continued frequenting the Coffee House for nearly more than a decade, till the late '60s, after he left college.

It was in the '70s that he would find it immensely difficult to get time away from his exceedingly busy schedule. His college friends were also becoming busier in their personal and professional lives. New groups replaced them and thronged the never-empty seats of the Coffee House. However, even in the '60s, Soumitra was a veritable star who would have feared being mobbed by the young, college-going crowd.

'I made it a point that I would never give an autograph to anyone while sitting with my group in the Coffee House. People knew this and no one approached as such. If someone unknowing of this would approach me, my friends took the onus on themselves to let the person know of my stance. Inside the Coffee House, I never wanted to carry any sort of star hangover. I wanted to be like any other friend of mine. And I think most people accepted me for that.

'I never cared for any fragile definition of heroism. I was alerted by many in the film industry, including Uttam Kumar and Suchitra Sen, for being casual about stardom. I was never unconfident of my acting skills, nor my image and stardom,' Soumitra said. Needless to say, Soumitra's stardom kept growing as he glowed with natural eloquence and simplicity.

***

Apart from literature and politics, the other topic that used to rock the Coffee House tables was theatre. It was Gourmohan Mukherjee again who left another indelible impact on Soumitra's mind by initiating him to the theatre of Sisir Kumar Bhaduri. It was with *Alamgir*—written by Kshirodprasad Vidyavinod, acted and directed by Sisir Kumar Bhaduri—that Soumitra's induction to the Bengali stage started. Sisir Kumar was the doyen of Bengali stage at that time, though he was a fading maestro, a fatigued legend who was almost made to retire from theatre for several inappropriate reasons in a few years' time.

Soumitra's chance to watch Sisir Kumar happened in the very first year itself. Like many who had witnessed Sisir Kumar on stage, Soumitra left in a trance. He had never experienced anything of this sort before. Even at a mature age, he maintained his admiration for the thespian and often commented that the reason he was never overawed by the overbearing senior actors of cinema—including Chhabi Biswas—was that he was tutored by none other than Sisir Kumar at the start of his acting career.

What was the uniqueness of Sisir Kumar's acting that held Soumitra captive throughout his life? Soumitra explained it with respect to Sisir Kumar's portrayal of Jibananda in Saratchandra

Chatterjee's popular play, *Soroshi*. It was a hugely successful adaptation and Sisir Kumar revived it again in the last phase of his career, when Soumitra got a chance to watch it. Sisir Kumar was well past sixty at the time but equally evocative in the romantic scenes with the heroine, Alaka.

Soumitra recounts, 'His portrayal of Jibananda aptly sums up Sisir Kumar's style of acting. In the scenes where he was holding debates in the village temple courtyard or when he was suffering from severe liver ailment, his acting was extremely natural. Watching those acts, one would feel transported to that time and place. Yet, in the romantic scenes with Alaka, when he would ask her in the most remorseful way, "Will you not return, Alaka?", it no longer remained merely naturalistic. It was imbibed with an adequate theatricality that transcended that acting moment to a different experience altogether.

'This confluence of different styles of acting was not very commonplace at that time... In Bengali theatre, there were three prominent streams of acting. One was extremely rhythmic, almost like having a singing style of dialogue delivery. Amritalal Mitra was a significant exponent of that style which was influenced by 'jatra', the traditional folk theatre. The other extreme was that of a superbly naturalistic style of acting practised by Ardhendu Sekhar Mustafi and, later, by Jogesh Choudhuri. Then there was a third stream which married both these extreme styles and brought in a balance of both. Girish Ghosh was a pioneer in this, followed by Sisir Kumar.'*

---

* Anasua Roy Choudhury, *Aaj Kaal Porshur Prante*, Krantik, 2000, pp. 50-51—translated by the author.

More than three decades later, Soumitra played the same character, Jibananda, for a television serial, where he tried to bring in the same pathos that he could remember in Sisir Kumar, without imitating the legend. Soumitra's maternal grandmother was still alive at that time. A huge fan of Sisir Kumar, she had witnessed most plays of the doyen. 'While the serial was on air for months, I deliberately didn't show any interest to find out from my Dida how she evaluated my portrayal. I knew she was comparing me with Sisir Kumar in her mind. Later, she told me that I had done a good job. To me, that was like passing the examination with distinction.' Soumitra loved recollecting this story in private discussions. Not to boast of his performance but to bask with utmost satisfaction in the glory of living up to the responsibility of being Sisir Kumar's disciple.

However, the duty and obligation to measure up to his mentor's fame was an acid test that Soumitra endured when he acted alongside Sisir Kumar, albeit only once. Sisir Kumar established his own theatre, Srirangam (later known as Biswaroopa), in 1942 and took it to popular heights with hit performances. Yet, after a decade or so, Sisir Kumar's theatre was plagued with problems and distractions till Srirangam was finally closed down on 24 January 1956. It was Girish Ghosh's legendary play, *Prafulla*, with which curtains were brought down on the theatre riddled with debts and hounded by moneylenders.

Ironical as it may seem, the last dialogues of the play, mouthed by Jogesh, played by Sisir Kumar, were, 'The garden that I tended for so many years has now faded and waned.' Soumitra was among the audience that very night. His Coffee

House friend, Ardhendu's mother Shefalika (Putul), was an actress in Sisir Kumar's group. A year or two later, she acted as Apu's mother-in-law in Soumitra's first role in Satyajit Ray's *Apur Sansar* (*The World of Apu*, 1959). It was she who took a young Soumitra to Sisir Kumar. It was a dream come true for Soumitra who had tried a few times earlier to meet Sisir Kumar but was always declined an appointment by the people surrounding the actor.

The environment within the green room was pensive; even the likes of Chhabi Biswas were stunned to silence by the inevitable reality that Sisir Kumar would not be on stage again. Sisir Kumar bade farewell that day but granted Soumitra permission to visit him at his residence on B.T. Road in North Calcutta.

Soumitra did visit Sisir Kumar but months later, on 2 October, the same year. It was Sisir Kumar's birthday. Soumitra visited him with two other friends and the trio was astounded to find Sisir Kumar lonely, pensive, friendless at his small flat. Soon after, Soumitra visited again, and friendship started to bloom between the two men despite the huge difference in their ages. The camaraderie flourished with discussions on theatre and literature. Sisir Kumar was an excellent speaker and Soumitra, an ardent listener.

Books were the vehicle of friendship; they shared what they read whenever Soumitra frequented Sisir Kumar, which was at least once every week. Soumitra's flair for language was soon noticed and on Sisir Kumar's insistence, Soumitra wrote his first adapted and translated play, *Bidhi o Byatikram*, based on Bertolt Brecht's *Exception and the Rule*. It was Sisir Kumar who initiated Soumitra to Brecht in the '50s, much before Brecht was yet to be popular with the Calcutta audience and playwrights alike. For Soumitra, the practice of adapting foreign plays and Indianizing them started with this undertaking.

A few months later, in his diary page dated 28 February 1957, Sisir Kumar would regard Soumitra as 'a likely merit for the stage'. On more than one occasion, he would lament that Soumitra came to him quite late and he didn't have a space to mentor Soumitra. The chance did come, once, when Soumitra acted as Suresh against Sisir Kumar's Jogesh in *Prafulla* at the Banga Sanskriti Sammelan at Marcus Square in 1957. Soumitra always maintained that the rehearsals for the few months were worth years in acting schools.

Sisir Kumar discouraged imitating his style because he believed that art begins where imitation ends. While handing over the script, Sisir Kumar provided Soumitra with a gem of an advice—to read a script like a detective, to look for hidden streams, to identify the missing texts unseen between the lines. Sisir Kumar believed that there existed a bigger, more profound play beyond the staged one and the role of an actor was to find and relate with it. Soumitra took this lesson to heart and followed it in his later career in cinema.

It was Sisir Kumar who trained Soumitra to throw his voice to different depths, to make his rendition loud yet free. Soumitra's voice was light at that time; Sisir Kumar insisted that he had a powerful voice but unfortunately, he was not aware of its strengths. Sisir Kumar would emphasize that his disciples understand the deeper meanings of a dialogue and then bring that out in their own individual characteristics. He would explain the subtexts and create a very sensitive emotional graph for the actors in order to grasp the inner logic of the characters. When he arrived on the silver screen for the first couple of films, Soumitra carried a detailed subtext of the characters and their activities when not shown on screen. Considering Sisir Kumar as his guru, Soumitra believed that the former's greatest strength was in being a facilitator, a guide showing the path for any young actor to tread his own journey.

On stage, acting alongside Sisir Kumar was quite a nerve-wracking affair. Soumitra remembered later how, in one scene when Jogesh (played by Sisir Kumar) thundered at Suresh (played by Soumitra), asking him to stop drinking, Soumitra would almost literally flee from the stage shattered by the impact of Sisir Kumar's evocative expression. Nivanani Devi, who was playing Jogesh's mother's character, was sitting near the wings. Watching Soumitra beat a hasty retreat and his anguish, Nivanani Devi proffered a piece of advice that Soumitra found earnest and fervent. She explained that they all were disciples of the legend, Sisir Kumar, and they should never commit this mistake of being bulldozed by the weight of a co-actor. Fortunately for Soumitra, it was a great lesson, one that he always followed in the initial years of his career while acting with some of the greatest in the Bengali film industry.

***

Meanwhile, Soumitra had already decided that he would study Bengali literature for his undergraduate honours, his romance with institutional science learning over by then.

Watching Sisir Kumar's acting instilled in him the belief and the unfurling ambition of taking up acting as a profession. To be an actor, one needed to know his mother language well enough; Soumitra used to think likewise. The wish to study the Bengali language with methodical planning made him pursue this dream.

At home, aspirations of acting were not rebuked but at the same time were not encouraged. Like any middle-class family, concerns over a potential money-earning future loomed large. Sambit, who was a brilliant student and already working, convinced their father Mohit Kumar that Soumitra should be left to do what he wished. Soumitra always acknowledged that this gesture of his brother—who was not even two years older than him—gave him immense comfort and assurance to chase his dreams. It also made him focus more—to prove his mettle and not to let Sambit down.

However, in order to make himself useful financially, after completing Bengali honours in 1955, Soumitra joined the Indo-Nepal Trading corporation, a private organization, as a probationary officer. He was soon promoted to the post of manager in the Cossipore Grinding Mill unit of the company. But Soumitra's tenure lasted only a few months. Once the results of the honours examination were published, Soumitra enrolled himself in the master's class of the Post-Graduate College of Arts in the Bengali department. Having enrolled for Master of Arts, Soumitra studied for two years but even before sitting for the final examination in 1957, he got a job in All India Radio as an announcer.

There is a little precursor to this story of Soumitra's first legitimate employment. Radio was an inseparable part of middle-class life at that time. Soumitra's house was no exception. Soumitra would marvel at the different voices he listened to. Being a reciter of poetry from a young age and an aspiring actor, he was certainly drawn to some of the most definitive voices of radio at that time. In the higher classes of school, he would take part in the immensely popular 'Golpo-dadur asor' (Grandpa's story party).

It was in late 1956 when Soumitra visited AIR again, this time as a job applicant for the post of an announcer. On the day of the audition and interview, to Soumitra's horror, he found a few hundred candidates for that solitary vacancy. He soon became friends with Anil Chatterjee, a handsome, fair man, five years senior to him. Anil was an assistant director in the film industry, a part-time actor, waiting for the big break in his life. After a few weeks, Soumitra got the offer from AIR. He joined immediately and came to know that he was second in the list. The original appointment letter had gone to Anil Chatterjee, who declined it since he had already received an offer to play a hero in cinema.

Anil Chatterjee went on to become an important actor for a few decades and only a few years from then, both Anil and Soumitra acted together in Satyajit Ray's *Devi* in 1960. Soumitra was with AIR for roughly more than a year and finally left it when he was to debut in cinema as Apu in Satyajit Ray's *Apur Sansar*. At AIR, Soumitra had to wait for long durations for announcements between songs. Restless as he was, it coached him in nurturing his patience, a training that helped him in future while waiting between shots of a film.

A very young Soumitra Chatterjee
(Photo Credit: Poulami Chatterjee)

Eventually, Soumitra got an offer from Delhi as a newsreader. But he had already thought deeply about the offer and decided to remain in Calcutta to pursue his dream of being an actor on the Bengali stage. Staying close to his Bengali roots to continue his creative quests in lieu of more lucrative prospects materially remained a constant with him all his life. As a successful actor later, he would never venture out of his beloved city to try his luck in foreign pastures, which would have definitely helped him financially.

In those halcyon days of uninhibited youth, visiting Sisir Kumar, spending time in the Coffee House, writing poetry, Soumitra and his friends formed a theatre group named 'Chhayanat' and staged occasional plays. Back at Calcutta

University, there was an inter-college theatre competition which was won by the team that represented the Post-Graduate College of Arts. Soumitra was an active part of it.

Subsequently, there was an Inter-University Youth Festival in Delhi where the Calcutta University team was represented by the best actors of different colleges. Before leaving for Delhi, the team was mentored for a month and a half by acting legend Ahindra Choudhury, who was the principal of the Academy of Dance and Drama, which later became Rabindra Bharati University. The Calcutta University team staged a one-act play based on W.W. Jacobs's supernatural story, *The Monkey's Paw*. Their production was awarded the second prize. Icing on the cake, as it may seem, Soumitra and his co-actor, Susanta Banerjee, were jointly given the best-actor award.

***

Year 1955—an epoch-making event happened that somehow changed the course of Bengali cinema, influenced Indian cinema too, and also, in a sense, defined Soumitra's future. It was the release of *Pather Panchali* by Satyajit Ray. Soumitra and his Coffee House comrades were blown away, watching the film back-to-back for a few days at a stretch. Soumitra had been an avid filmgoer since childhood. But his staple was Hollywood films and a handful of Pramathesh Barua's. Sisir Kumar was extremely sceptical about cinema himself, sparing only Charlie Chaplin from his wrath. Soumitra was not very forgiving as well as far as Bengali cinema was concerned.

The 1952 international film festival at Calcutta, the first of its kind, also had an impact on Soumitra and his Coffee House friends. They watched Vittoria de Sica's *Bicycle Thieves* and *Miracle in Milan*, apart from a few other masterpieces—films that seized their imagination. Three years later, it was *Pather Panchali* that bolstered Soumitra's belief in cinema being an intellectual entertainment. Post the success of the film, there was a felicitation programme for the entire cast and crew at the Senate Hall in Calcutta. That was the first time that Soumitra and his friends witnessed Satyajit Ray in person.

Most of the speakers praised *Pather Panchali* and emphasized how the film denounced all commercial elements found in typical Indian films at that time. Ray was the last speaker of the day. Soumitra recalled how Ray was absolutely clear in his opinion that cinema being a collaborative art form with a producer investing in the director's idea and vision, he had always been careful about not squandering it with his fanciful experimentations. Satyajit insisted that he didn't wish to make a film for only his near ones. He wanted his film to reach more and more people as he believed that his films could shine with the audience as well as offer more refined entertainment than the commonplace and mundane.

'My friends and I were surprised to hear such an honest confession. We realized at that moment that this man was a creative persona of a completely different breed, one who would almost singlehandedly carve his own path and carry Bengali cinema to a previously uncharted domain. There was a different stirring in my mind since that speech in the Senate Hall.'*

---

* Arunendra Mukherjee, *Naam Soumitra*, Arkadeep, 1995, p. 35— translated by the author.

For the next two-three years, watching every new Ray film was a custom, soaking in the remarkable style of 'non-acting' that Ray's cinema exhibited with precision. It was a style which Ray was carving slowly but surely, freeing cinema acting from the theatrical melodrama that had thrived in Bengali cinema till then. The biggest proponent of this style, the most perfect brand ambassador of this, was meanwhile getting ready silently, in the dark interiors of cinema halls in Calcutta.

THREE

A Golden Streak

Soumitra didn't have to wait long to meet Satyajit Ray in person after that Senate Hall felicitation. It was shortly before Ray embarked upon the journey to make his second film, *Aparajito*, the sequel to *Pather Panchali*. Soumitra was staying at their Mirzapur Street residence at that time. It was walking distance from the College Street Coffee House. One day, while he was on his way to visit the Coffee House, he met his friend Tapan. Tapan soon engaged Soumitra in very inconsequential small talk. Soumitra could sense that he was also signalling to someone on the opposite footpath. Soon, Tapan's act was discovered.

His collaborator was Nityananda Datta who happened to be an assistant in Satyajit Ray's unit. Tapan and Nityananda explained that they were scouting for an actor to play the young Apu in Ray's film and asked whether Soumitra would be interested. The news about Ray's next film being *Aparajito* was already known by then. Soumitra and his friends, who were appreciative of *Pather Panchali*, had been anxiously curious about his next venture. No wonder then that Soumitra didn't bat an eyelid in agreeing to meet Ray.

He immediately boarded a bus with Nityananda and went to Ray's house. Soumitra recalled, 'The moment I entered Mr Ray's room, he told me, "Oh-ho, you are a bit taller than my conception of Apu." I was amazed by his single-minded focus on the subject. Evidently, he was so immersed in the film that this was what he said to me at our very first meeting! He then talked to me in a general way, asking what I did, etc. But I was not cast as Apu in *Aparajito*!'*

Aparajito went on to win the Golden Lion at the Venice Film Festival and followed it up with quite a few awards at different film festivals across the globe. Though he missed out on playing Apu in *Aparajito*, Soumitra kept himself updated about Satyajit Ray's cinematic endeavours.

However, the first attempt to work in cinema happened even before Ray chose Soumitra to play Apu. It was in 1957 and Kartick Chatterjee was then auditioning for the role of Chaitanyadeb for his religious venture, *Neelachale Mahaprabhu*. Soumitra was rejected in the screen test and the role went to Asim Kumar, who rose to instant stardom with this maiden venture. The film was a big hit and travelled the country with dubbing and subtitles. The loss didn't deter Soumitra much since he was not extremely keen on playing the role of a religious crusader. His friends had insisted that Soumitra appear for the screen test, given his marked handsome looks.

---

* Amitava Nag, *Beyond Apu: 20 Favourite Film Roles of Soumitra Chatterjee*, HarperCollins Publishers, India, 2016, p. 2.

Subir Hajra, one of Ray's assistants, was Soumitra's friend at the Coffee House. Hajra used to tell him that Ray had kept him in mind and would call him as and when a suitable role was available. Soumitra found no reason to believe Hajra, thinking this was Satyajit Ray's way of humouring him. It was when Ray was making *Paras Pathar* and *Jalsaghar* that Soumitra went down with chickenpox. After he recovered, Ray summoned him once again and Soumitra paid him a visit. Ray was afraid that the ailment had left permanent scars on Soumitra's face. He was relieved to find nothing problematic. This meeting was a longer one than the first and Ray enquired if Soumitra was still interested in acting.

The lure of acting was raging within Soumitra at that time, thanks to his frequent interactions with Sisir Kumar Bhaduri. Ray wished to find out if Soumitra had any prior acting experience. Soumitra had none in films but he mentioned his association with Sisir Kumar. It was during this meeting that Ray declared his wish to make the third part of the Apu trilogy. He further stated that Soumitra may be cast in some role after a couple of essential voice and camera tests were performed.

Particular as he was, Ray asked Soumitra what he would do with his day job in All India Radio should he act in the film. Soumitra instantly replied that he would leave the job to do the film. In hindsight, it was an emotional decision but not completely impractical or illogical. Soumitra was deeply influenced by his mentor, Sisir Kumar Bhaduri, at that time, who—at the peak of his career—had left his secure job as a college professor.

'At that spur of the moment, I thought if Sisir Kumar

could forego such a safe profession for the sake of his theatre, why couldn't I do it for cinema?' Soumitra recounted later in discussions. He left the job a few days before the shooting of *Apur Sansar* commenced.

That day Soumitra left with the promise of keeping in touch with Ray but unsure about the role Ray had in mind for him. Ray invited him to visit the studio and the sets of two films—*Paras Pathar* and *Jalsaghar*—the ones he was working on at that time simultaneously. It was the set of *Paras Pathar* that Soumitra visited first and a whole new world of cinema started opening up. The detailed intricacies of step-by-step building up of a make-believe world, the role of camera and lighting, became points of interest for Soumitra.

It was the famous party scene in *Paras Pathar* with a galaxy of stars and actors of Bengali cinema that Soumitra witnessed unfolding before him. He started understanding the nuances of film acting and identifying the differences with acting in theatre, which was till then his nurturing ground. Only later on did he realize that Ray had facilitated these experiences only to put him at ease and make him less self-conscious before the camera.

It was on one such occasion when Soumitra visited the shooting of *Jalsaghar* that Satyajit Ray formally introduced him to the legendary Chhabi Biswas, declaring then and there that Soumitra would be playing Apu in the next and last part of the trilogy. Dumbfounded, Soumitra was caught completely unawares. On his way back to office at AIR, his head started reeling in excitement. He wished that the bus had wings to carry him faster and yearned to shout out to the world that Satyajit Ray had chosen him to play Apu. Much later, Soumitra came to know from Ray's family that Ray had decided to make the third part of Apu right after meeting Soumitra the very first time; the screen and voice tests along with making him familiar with the shooting environment within a studio were mere formalities.

Soumitra now started visiting the then Ray house at Lake View Road. Like he did in most cases, Ray took a number of still photographs of Soumitra and asked him to read Bibhuti Bhushan Banerjee's *Aparajito* once more to understand the multifarious identities of an adult Apu. But more than preparing Soumitra for the role of Apu alone, Ray probably took up the onus of tutoring him to be a good actor in general, which would stand him in good stead even later.

The duo discussed acting techniques. Soumitra had already read Konstantin Stanislavski's *My Life in Art* and *Building a Character*—two seminal books on acting theory. It was Stanislavski's *An Actor Prepares* that Soumitra hadn't studied till then. Ray lent his own copy and advised Soumitra to read it thoroughly, mentioning that it was the best guide for any beginner. The other suggestion Ray made to Soumitra was to read *Film Technique and Film Acting* by famous Russian director, V.I. Pudovkin, who pioneered, amongst others, the great Russian montage techniques.

***

Exchange of ideas and information on books happened between them, much like the way it used to be between Soumitra and Sisir Kumar. However, in that exchange, Soumitra acted more as a provider of books to an ailing and aged Sisir Kumar wishing to revisit the ones he had already read, and the newer, contemporary ones suggested by a young Soumitra. With Ray, it was more of a structured reading for the actor-to-be as he would borrow books on various subjects from Ray's personal collection or from other sources following Ray's reference. Soumitra's natural hunger for reading was fanned by the mentoring of two superlative geniuses.

Ray's grooming went beyond trading books alone. He would discuss Hollywood films and emphasize on specific acting moments, drawing Soumitra's attention to the finer nuances. At times, Ray would ask Soumitra to accompany him to morning shows in cinema halls. Soumitra remembered watching Billy Wilder's *Lost Weekend* together at the Basusree cinema hall one Sunday morning. Ray insisted Soumitra take note of Ray Milland's acting as a definitive example of cinema acting.

On the last day of the shooting of *Jalsaghar*, Ray took a screen test of Soumitra. He was happy with the output and found Soumitra confident about facing the camera. A voice test followed soon after. Soumitra had been a reciter and elocutionist since his school days, being influenced by his father and grandfather. While in college, he used to participate in programmes and literary events as an elocutionist. Ray came to know of this aspect and asked him to recite a poem for the voice test. Soumitra recited Rabindranath Tagore's 'Banshi', a rendition Ray liked immensely. It is a simple conjecture that the couple of short spurts of recitation in *Apur Sansar*, then in *Charulata* and further in *Ghare Baire*, were all dictated by Soumitra's natural flair for the spoken word—which Ray utilized fittingly.

The act of preparing for the role was two-pronged. Firstly, Soumitra started analysing acting in different films, Hollywood as well as Ray's own, and began to fathom the nuances of natural acting. Ray's cinema, in particular, provides a platter of what may be termed as 'non-acting'. He soon realized the importance of discontinuity in a film actor's work, which was different from that of a stage actor. Also, the role of camera in bringing the human face and figure closer to or away from the screen or audience, depending on the shot selection.

At that early age, Soumitra could understand the technical differences between acting in cinema and on stage and then in television, decades later. Watching Ray at work helped Soumitra translate the concepts in theory to actual actions in practice.

Secondly, Soumitra was warming up to play Apu in particular. For only a few sequences, he would take flute lessons from Pandit Gour Goswami who was famous as 'The Bengal Tiger of the bamboo flute'. Additionally, Ray provided Soumitra with a two-page character analysis of Apu and the complete script of *Apur Sansar* well in advance. He had never before given any other actor the complete script to prepare.

Soumitra was enthralled by Ray's poetic script in English and was fascinated by the accompanying character analysis. There were revealing aspects in it, like Apu's sexual attraction towards Aparna being one of the possible causes for his agreeing to marry her on the spur of the moment. Soumitra himself came up with a subtext describing an action map of Apu even when he was off-screen. Ray was impressed by Soumitra's meticulous preparations and the duo would occasionally debate over some probable actions of Apu.

Ray was careful about a new actor's problems in maintaining narrative continuity and expressing a linear thematic character progression in a disjointed and nonlinear shooting schedule. More so if someone was trained in theatre, which had lesser discontinuities. Accordingly, wherever possible, he would let Soumitra rehearse the long dialogues and try out a few times on location before the final take. The scene along the railway yard in the beginning of the film—when Pulu first takes Apu out for a sumptuous meal—was one such.

Later on, Soumitra could recollect with precision how he and Swapan Mukherjee, who played Pulu, would rehearse that long scene on the India Film Laboratories shooting floor and then at the real location before the actual shoot. Zoom lenses were not available at that time, the push trolly was not sufficiently close to the characters and in the editing room, Ray would later punch a few close-tracking shots captured in the studio. For Soumitra, the studio close-up shots were a challenge—without the co-actor, the realism of the location, the artificially created night light and an absolute disparate ambience. It was through acting these scenes in his very first film itself that Soumitra could better understand how the writings and teachings of Pudovkin could be applied in practice.

Beleghata CIT Road, Calcutta, 9 August 1958. The scene involved Apu going to a bottling and labelling factory for work but being sufficiently disillusioned by the abject nature of the profession. Soumitra Chatterjee first stood in front of the camera. The very first shot was an OK in the first take itself. Ray was happy.

An association began between the two—a maestro already

and a genius in the making. Their working relationship continued through his fourteen feature films with Ray, apart from several other associations. More importantly, in Soumitra, Bengali cinema finally found a leading man who didn't blink an eye at breaking his image to play any worthy character. Soumitra's journey continued onscreen for six decades; he became a part of the Bengali existence, a source of sustenance for the Bengali psyche much more than any of his contemporaries. In carving a punctilious path in the different realms of art—including literature, painting and theatre—apart from cinema, Soumitra remains unparalleled. A luminary, an exception.

***

Soumitra had several stories to recollect about *Apur Sansar*. But there were three that topped his lists every time he would set out to reveal them. First was shooting the sequence where Apu would meet Pulu for the last time in a coalmine and the latter would persuade Apu to go back and take care of Kajal, his son. Apu was supposed to be tired—mentally, because of the emotional ride he had gone through, and physically, since he had to run up and down the uneven geography of the place to meet Pulu.

Accordingly, Ray asked Soumitra to bring in the expression of breathlessness to his acting. A naïve Soumitra actually ran up and down the terrain to make the acting realistic, only to go down with a medical condition later that evening. Ray liked the sincerity of the young actor who was earnest about overcoming the inexperience of his acting techniques at that time.

The second one was a rather indelible experience for the artist in Soumitra. After Aparna's death, there were shots of Apu wandering in the forests, which were filmed in Netarhat. It was an overnight journey from Howrah to Muri by train and onwards to Ranchi. Soumitra shared a first-class coupé on the train to Muri with Satyajit Ray. They would arrive at Muri early in the morning and that night, neither of the two slept as they discussed different art forms, but mostly cinema. It was Soumitra's chance of speaking to Ray at length, undisturbed, and he clarified all his doubts about the art and craft of cinema. Those exchanges remained with Soumitra throughout, whenever he would direct his actors on stage or the lone Doordarshan film he made in 1986 called *Stree Ka Patra*, to commemorate Rabindranath Tagore's 125th birth anniversary.

The third was one of personal gratification. Satyajit Ray had made a big poster of Charlie Chaplin's *Limelight* when it was released in Calcutta. It was put up at Chowringhee crossing. Later, when *Apur Sansar* was released, the Chaplin poster was replaced by another of Ray's that had Apu's bearded face on it. Seeing his own face so big and wide on the streets for the first time was a thrilling experience for Soumitra and his friends of the Coffee House.

Apur Sansar was released on 1 May 1959 and was an instant success. Soumitra became the talk of the town immediately. Only Radhamohan Bhattacharjee in *Udayer Pathe* (1944) following up with its Hindi remake, *Hamrahi* (1945), had become such a successful star overnight. Critics were generous and soon, Soumitra was approached by another doyen of Indian cinema, Tapan Sinha, for the role of the hero in Sinha's second attempt at a Tagore story, *Kshudhita Pashan*.

Throughout his life, Ray was Soumitra's mentor and advisor, a confidant and a source of sustenance. Soumitra approached Ray for his advice, to which Ray emphasized that Soumitra should take up other directors' offers and Tapan Sinha was indeed one of the finest around. In between, Soumitra also signed a contract for *Sasti*, by Dayabhai, which was completed and released a few years later.

The one director apart from Ray for whom Soumitra had utmost respect and who reciprocated his admiration for Soumitra's art effusively was Tapan Sinha. Sinha was a master craftsman who had his training in London and worked as a sound recordist in the New Theatres studio before graduating to a director. An avid follower of Hollywood films, Sinha was a dedicated student of filmmaking techniques and an excellent tutor of film acting.

Satyajit Ray had almost always given Soumitra enough liberty in his films in terms of acting. He had this unique style of letting the intelligent actor internalize the role and behave in accordance. It was Sinha who essentially taught Soumitra some of the finer aspects of film-acting, starting with the walk. How a hero must walk gracefully and yet manly. In *Kshudhita Pashan*, there were scenes of long walks by the hero through the corridors of the ancient princely mansion. Sinha had the set built well in advance; he made Soumitra rehearse the long walks and get familiar with the sets. It helped Soumitra act in those scenes effortlessly and also marked out his distinct walking style.

In personal recollections, Soumitra elaborated how Tapan Sinha would show the movement of hands while walking, the distance between the feet which would give a good rhythm, the position of the shoulders and how the head should remain still. Not only that, Sinha also guided Soumitra on how to relax within his acting and the postures of resting during the long intervals between two shots.

Soumitra himself realized that to be a professional actor and to appear as a hero in films, an elegant gait was essential, apart from a handsome face and features. He would observe the animal grace of many a sportsperson on field and the workmanlike power among workers and farmers. At a young age, when he visited his father in Rajasthan during a vacation, Soumitra would observe how women would carry a series of vessels containing water on their heads and walk for miles in the desert. To Soumitra, there was no better spectacle of human poise while walking than the Rajput women carrying water on their heads.

Ever since he decided to become an actor, Soumitra practised walking with a pile of books on his head. However, Tapan Sinha taught him a scientific and accurate lesson about how to walk for a long time with the same natural freshness. Not only with walking, Sinha arranged for Soumitra to take trainings at the Society of Horsemanship and Equestrianism since there were a few scenes of him riding horses in *Kshudhita Pashan*. Soon, this training paid off when Soumitra pulled off one of the finest characterisations as the villain Mayurbahan in Sinha's *Jhinder Bandi*.

It was during the shooting of *Kshudhita Pashan* that Soumitra first became professionally acquainted with Chhabi Biswas. Soumitra had met Biswas earlier on the sets of *Jalsaghar* when Satyajit Ray had introduced him to the acting legend. Chhabi Biswas was already the biggest name in Bengali cinema at that time. There were glaring rumours about his mood swings, tantrums and tendencies to overshadow fellow actors on screen. Soumitra was not unaware of these and on the first day of shooting with Biswas, he went to him and completely surrendered himself—'Kindly teach me when I go wrong.'

Biswas liked Soumitra instantly and soon a bonding developed between the actors of disparate age groups. Soumitra had almost always been like a soft sponge soaking in all the teachings—direct verbal ones or by observing others—throughout his life. Biswas insisted that one of the major factors of good acting was confidence and more importantly, there could be multifarious interpretations in expressing a role. 'What I may think wrong could be another way of looking at it,' Biswas told Soumitra.

Though the shooting of *Kshudhita Pashan* started earlier, it was Satyajit Ray's *Devi* which was released before and hence credited as Soumitra's second film. In both these films, Soumitra had a chance to act with Chhabi Biswas and learn the varied acting skills from him. They shared a cordial relationship and for Soumitra, every opportunity of acting together was a gift. The third and final appearance together was in Ajoy Kar's *Atal Jaler Ahwan* in 1962. Unlike the previous two, in this film, Soumitra had more scenes with Chhabi Biswas.

Biswas had a phenomenal memory and could recite long Sanskrit verses at ease just by reading them a few times, to the disbelief of others. Soumitra had been a witness to that while shooting in *Devi* where Biswas had to deliver verses from Kalidasa's *Raghuvansham* and he did it with effortless ease. However, on the very first day of shooting in *Atal Jaler Ahwan*, Soumitra found a distraught, distracted and fretful Biswas forgetting even simpler dialogues and getting angry with almost everyone around.

Soumitra observed that with all the make-up on, it was very difficult for Biswas to rehearse the dialogues in the sweltering heat. He suggested the doyen to take off the make-up, be cool and then rehearse again. Soumitra even went forward, to the disbelief of others around, and pointed out to Biswas where he was making a mistake. It was a daring act for a newcomer to call attention to the problems in someone like Chhabi Biswas's acting. But Biswas was magnanimous in accepting the suggestion and the shot went off well.

It was later, during a break in the day's shooting, that Soumitra found a lonely, forlorn Chhabi Biswas contemplating retirement. An utterly pained Soumitra could only ask why he was leaving his kingdom and the throne of Bengali cinema which he so richly deserved. Chhabi Biswas was a witty person and would comment then, winking at Soumitra, that a prince was already in the making.

Soumitra recalled another incident of learning from Chhabi Biswas. It was the same film and this time, it was he who was unable to deliver a part of the dialogue with the desired effect. Biswas was observing this for a while but didn't comment till Soumitra went up to him and requested him to tell him where he was going wrong. Biswas enquired if Soumitra had Biswas's dialogues by heart and also his movements. Soumitra felt pride in telling him that he did note all his actions and had memorized Biswas's dialogues, apart from his own.

Biswas instructed Soumitra to enact his part and he would then do Soumitra's. To his disbelief, Soumitra found out that Biswas also had the entire dialogue sheet of Soumitra memorized. Biswas showed where Soumitra was going wrong and affectionately commented, 'Learn, learn, when else will you otherwise.'

Chhabi Biswas didn't live long after that, passing away in a car accident on 11 June 1962 shortly after *Atal Jaler Ahwan* was released. It was an irreparable loss for Bengali cinema and personally for Soumitra as well, who would miss an acting mentor who was an actor himself, and that too of the highest calibre. Only after Biswas's untimely death did Soumitra realize how Biswas had been mindful of his talents.

During the shooting of *Atal Jaler Ahwan*, Chhabi Biswas would advise Soumitra time and again to continue acting in theatre because that was where the real talent of an actor gets nurtured. Biswas earnestly believed that a stint in theatre would mature Soumitra faster as a professional actor. After Biswas passed away, Soumitra was contracted to play the lead role of Dipak in *Tapasi*, directed by Debnarayan Gupta, at the Star Theatre.

Starting with the first stage show on 14 February 1963, *Tapasi* was a runaway hit for two years at a stretch with nearly five hundred performances, though Soumitra had to leave it after a hundred-odd for Satyajit Ray's *Charulata*. The contract with Star Theatre happened soon after Biswas's death. Soumitra was taken to the make-up room well before the rehearsals—it was the one where Chhabi Biswas used to do his make-up when he was with Star Theatre. The room was kept locked after Biswas's demise, opened only for Soumitra. But more importantly, unknown to Soumitra, Chhabi Biswas had insisted that they give Soumitra a contract. He explained that the gain would have been mutual—Star would have got a new and promising hero and Soumitra would find a hearth to sharpen his skills.

Till his last, Soumitra could never forget these golden touches of senior practitioners who guided him and helped him bloom to his fullest. It was in *Atal Jaler Ahwan* that Soumitra also became friends with Bhanu Banerjee and Jahar Roy, two of the finest comedy actors of Bengali cinema till date. Both became personal friends, with Bhanu sticking with Soumitra through thick and thin, mostly during the turbulent days of the industry in the last years of that decade. Observing them act, Soumitra would learn a lot about comic timing, which he would bring to his acting in comedy films later on.

***

Soumitra's ascension to glory is almost like a fairy tale. He would always admit that he was lucky to get the chances he had and the films that he would get to act in. In the first decade of his acting, the '60s, he acted in thirty-eight films in total, which included six of Satyajit Ray, five of Ajoy Kar, three each of Asit Sen and Mrinal Sen and two of Tapan Sinha. In comparison, Uttam Kumar, who was undoubtedly a bigger commercial star with more than fifty films in the same decade, had two of Satyajit Ray, two each of Ajoy Kar and Tapan Sinha and one of Asit Sen.

No other Bengali actor would command the same kind of respect from these eminent directors and provide them with an assurance of performance the way Soumitra Chatterjee could in roles that were realistic, closer to life and free from heroic mannerisms. On the one hand, he would be the romantic, innocent Amal in Ray's classic *Charulata*, the egoistic college teacher in Ajoy Kar's *Saat Paake Bandha* or the psychiatrist in the hilarious rom-com, *Bakso Badal*, by Nityananda Dutta. And on the other hand, he would be the Rajput taxi driver Narsingh in Satyajit Ray's *Abhijan*, the shrewd, sly imposter in Mrinal Sen's *Akash Kusum* or the urban ruffian adept at eve-teasing in Ashutosh Bandyopadhyay's *Teen Bhuvaner Paare*.

In Satyajit Ray's films alone, from *Abhijan* to *Charulata*, Soumitra could portray a rainbow of emotions and histrionic abilities. For *Charulata*, he had to change his handwriting for good in order to have an authentic pre-Tagore hand since Ray wanted to have multiple sequences showing Amal in the process of writing.

On a personal note, Soumitra had mixed feelings about *Charulata*. The film was released on 17 April 1964. It was his father's birthday and Mohit Kumar attended the premiere. This happened to be the last film featuring Soumitra that Mohit Kumar could watch. Not even a month later, on the 14th of May, he passed away. Mohit Kumar couldn't witness the heights his second son would scale in the future. Soumitra recalled in personal interactions how his father was secretly proud of his acting but would never openly acknowledge the same. Only after his passing away, when Soumitra met some of his father's friends, did he come to know how Mohit Kumar would bask in his son's acting glories. In his personal life as a father, Soumitra tried to imbibe this sense of restrained adulation for his children, fearing that otherwise, he would be a blind propagandist for them.

It was in 1961 that Soumitra was pitted as the villain Mayurbahan against the royal hero in a double role—played by Uttam Kumar—in Tapan Sinha's epic, *Jhinder Bandi*. It was indeed a casting coup of sorts; who could even think of breaking the innocent, dreamer image of Soumitra and cast him as a stunningly cruel and overtly manipulative Mayurbahan? When Tapan Sinha first introduced Soumitra to his cinema in *Kshudhita Pashan*, he consulted Ray before offering the role to Soumitra. With the experience of that one film, Sinha could gauge the depth of Soumitra's histrionic abilities before handing him one of the most dashing antiheroes of Indian cinema.

Needless to say, Soumitra grabbed the opportunity with both hands and delivered with aplomb. It was this film that cemented him as the most deserving rival of the legendary Uttam Kumar. The Uttam vs Soumitra binary was much like the one between Mohun Bagan and East Bengal, or the people of West Bengal and the migrants from the East, which flares and remains potent even today. In retrospect, it is unjust, and to a large extent, a misinterpretation of Soumitra's varied and illustrious body of work. No other Bengali actor can boast of the array of roles that Soumitra could essay—from being a young man to an octogenarian—over the last six decades.

But apart from the professional successes in cinema, the '60s were strewn with a number of personal joys as well. Two months after the release of his second feature film *Devi*,

Soumitra tied the knot on 18 April 1960 with his teenage love, Deepa. Deepa was Soumitra's sister Anuradha's friend and a known name in the household. Yet, the path to marriage wasn't a cakewalk for both the families. Primarily in Deepa's family since Soumitra's earnings from AIR were not substantial at that time. Later, becoming an actor didn't help either since in those days, joining the film industry was not considered noble and respectable. Deepa had already lost her mother and it was Soumitra's good looks and comely manners which finally won his in-laws' hearts.

Soumitra Chatterjee with his wife Deepa Chatterjee
(Photo Credit: Sukumar Roy)

The very next year, on 27 September 1961, Deepa and Soumitra's first child, Sougata (known as Bubu), was born. Four years later in the same month but on the fourth day, their second child arrived—Poulami aka Mithil. Sougata took an interest in Western classical music and grew to be an eloquent violin player apart from being a noted poet. Poulami took to dancing at a very young age under the tutelage of the legendary Thankamani Kutti. Apart from being a Bharatnatyam exponent, Poulami also trained in Mohiniyattam and Kathakali with Kalamandalam Venkit. She runs her own dance school and is now an eminent theatre director and actor on the Bengali stage.

Initiating her acting lessons under Utpal Dutt's guidance in plays including *Ekla Chalo Re*, *Aajker Shah Jahan* and *Baniker Mandondo*, she slowly but surely groomed herself under her legendary father in plays like *Atmakatha*, *Homapakhi*, *Neelkantha* and *Chhariganga*. Poulami is now the creative director of the theatre group, Shyambajar Mukhomukhi. Having acted under her father's direction, Poulami eventually went on to direct him in the remake versions of the immensely successful *Phera* and *Ghatak Biday*, where she acted as well.

Incidentally, it was for the role of Amulya in Satyajit Ray's *Samapti*, the third part of *Teen Kanya*, that Soumitra received the Best Actor award for the first time from the prestigious Bengal Film Journalists' Association (BFJA). Soumitra eventually went on to win it seven more times to become the most awarded actor.

The year 1961 was a remarkable one for Soumitra for another reason. He started to jointly edit the excellent literary magazine, *Ekshan*, with college friend Nirmalya Acharya.

Bringing out a literary magazine that would not only focus on stories, novels and poems but would also be a home of critical and analytical essays was the thinking behind *Ekshan*. Soumitra, Nirmalya and his friends had dreamt of such a magazine since they were in college and frequenting the Coffee House. Their friends, Sunil Ganguly and Shakti Chatterjee, were already bringing out the poetry magazine *Krittibas* and a section of the literary-minded youth was craving for a similar avenue for critical essays.

Soumitra was already a rising hero after the success of his first few films when one day in the evening, after their regular Coffee House session, Nirmalya broached the idea of realizing the dream. Soumitra was reluctant initially simply because his demanding professional life made him apprehensive of his participation in the editorial process. He didn't want to have his name added in the masthead only for his star status. Nirmalya was hell-bent on starting the magazine only if Soumitra decided to co-edit it.

Finally, it was Deepa who vetoed the idea of having a single editor of a collective dream. Soumitra took Nirmalya to Satyajit Ray, who gave the magazine its name—meaning 'Now'—whose first edition was published in April 1961 (actual Bengali calendar date on the magazine being Baisakh-Jaistho 1368). Ray designed the logo and drew the cover design of all the issues of the magazine, which lasted three decades! In the late 1980s, when Ray was physically incapacitated to draw new cover designs, the magazine recycled some of its older ones.

Also interesting to note is the fact that in the same year, 1961, Ray along with his poet friend Subhas Mukherjee revived

Sandesh, the literary magazine for children which had been started by his grandfather, Upendra Kishore Raychoudhuri, and later carried on by his father, Sukumar Ray. It was due to *Sandesh* that Ray took to writing seriously; it was here that he started penning his two famous characters, the scientist Professor Sonku and the detective Feluda, both of which in no time became an absolute craze amongst young adolescents.

A decade and a half later, Ray eventually made two films from his two novels on Feluda and cast Soumitra as the sleuth, one of the most iconic roles played by the actor. Several actors went on to play Feluda since Soumitra breathed life into him in *Sonar Kella* (1974) and *Joy Baba Felunath* (1979) but Soumitra remains, till date, the quintessential Feluda to all audiences for over four decades.

Ray was a guiding strength behind *Ekshan*, introducing the young editors to authors like Kamal Kumar Majumdar, allowing his own film scripts to be published for the first time and also by writing deep and provocative articles including '*Rabindrasangeet-a bhabar katha*' ('Things to ponder about Rabindra Sangeet'). Soon, *Ekshan* became a peerless magazine with special issues on Karl Marx and Dante being noteworthy. A host of writers who were typically non-mainstream—including the maverick Kamal Kumar Majumdar, Ashim Roy, Abhijit Sen, Amiyabhushan Majumdar—were all regular writers at *Ekshan*.

However, in retrospect, two specific duties that *Ekshan* never faltered in during the first two decades when Soumitra was associated with it were: building a canon of work of female writers of the nineteenth century, and secondly, reprinting important literature of the previous century that reflected the life and times of people in that era. The magazine republished the biography of Ardhendu Sekhar Mustafi, a contemporary of Girish Ghosh, and also a literary critique of Rangalal Banerjee.

Through these reprints, the magazine brought to light some of the lost jewels of the Bengali literary pantheon which would benefit researchers in their understanding of the cultural life of nineteenth-century Bengal. Parallely, the magazine also published memoirs of some of the prominent cultural personalities of the time—legendary dancer Uday Shankar, painter Somnath Hore, to name some. These memoirs, in contrast to the reprints, helped capture the contemporary times of the mid-1960s.

The first duty was indeed a progressive one in the context of the times as the editor duo published autobiographical works of women writers. Not only did they reprint yesteryear actress Binodini Dasi's autobiography, *Apon Katha* (Own Words), along with footnotes and annotations, but they also published a host of similar memoirs including, but not restricted to, Prasannamayi Devi's *Purbakatha* (Of Earlier Times), Manada Devi's *Janaika Grihabadhur Diary* (Diary of a Common Housewife), Jnanadanandini Devi's *Smritikatha* (Memoirs) and Saiyad Manoyara Khatun's *Smritir Pata* (From the Memory Pages). Ray's researcher Debasis Mukherjee hinted that in *Charulata*, for the sequences involving Charu's writings, Ray had extensively read and researched the memoirs of women writers of the nineteenth century. Probably, that homework directly or indirectly influenced Soumitra to take up the task of publishing these obsolete memoirs.

None of the contemporary magazines at that time

considered these two aspects so seriously—paying importance to a female voice in understanding and observing the socio-economic condition of contemporary life, and to play the role of an archivist in making available some of the important but extinct works of the previous century along with building a repository of contemporary writings for the future.

Soumitra played a very active and significant role as the co-editor of *Ekshan*—both in the planning and also in its execution. He used his connections to raise advertisements for the magazine, almost single-handedly. This included the few advertisements he appeared in, maintaining always that the remuneration he was owed would be paid to *Ekshan* and not to him. It is important to appreciate that for a budding hero for whom the individual glamour quotient must have been extremely vital, for whom every possible advice might always have been contrary to these so-called 'de-glamourizing' activities, it was a tremendous uphill challenge.

A magazine editor's role is always putting forward others' works ahead of one's own. For a cinema hero, the equations have always been the opposite. Soumitra's deep love for literature, his commitment to his friends and his passion for contributing selflessly to the history of Bengali literary culture were so ingrained that for him, the magazine's editorial work was never an exception. It followed naturally from his Coffee House days. Rather, it was as if being a rising star in Bengali cinema who acted in most of the better films throughout that one decade was an exception in itself.

This capacity of hiding the self and projecting the other in his editorial work probably provides an insight into why he always remained an actor first and not a hero with repetitive mannerisms. It was this mental map of Soumitra Chatterjee that enabled him to dig into a character as a flesh-and-blood human being instead of a paper-thin caricature of himself.

To understand the creative mind of Soumitra Chatterjee, the nuances of him being a cultural icon, we must keep in mind these parallel activities that kept him grounded. His poems, his prose writings, his editorial work and later his theatre (both adapting plays and then directing and acting in them), along with his unwavering support for Marxist ideology, nurtured Soumitra's fertile mental ground.

Soumitra Chatterjee didn't become a film actor with a difference, overnight. There is no other film actor in India, living or dead, who could be so meaningful and worthwhile with his or her continued deliverance for six decades. That Soumitra Chatterjee would become an inseparable identity of the Bengali psyche had its roots in his formative decade of the '60s. On one hand, he consolidated his position in Bengali cinema as the undisputed hero of the thinking man, and on the other, he strengthened his own creative resolve to be a unique horse in the cultural stable.

FOUR

Triumph and Turmoil

On the completion of twelve years in the Bengali film industry, Soumitra wrote an essay titled 'Swogoto' ('Soliloquy'), where he looked back at his journey in the film industry. The essay was immensely personal, all about his stupendous boredom working in film after film that had nothing substantial to offer him. Interestingly enough, he raised this disquiet after acting in quite a few better films of the previous decade, including the ones by Satyajit Ray, Mrinal Sen and Tapan Sinha.

Soumitra's complete disillusionment was not limited to the repetitive roles with nothing celebratory to offer. Rather, his disenchantment was against the entire power structure that prevailed then, and even now. His leftist political views made it uneasy for him to work in a system where he could understand that, 'I am an actor, I sell my hard work, my sweat and toil to carve out a fictional character onscreen. But all these efforts don't help in the daily hardship, relentless struggle for existence of my fellow Bengalis. This is because those who buy my hard work and my creativity don't approve of my desires, my ideologies, my mentality. They only sieve my capacity to act in a role. And they do business with that. Hence, there's a gap between my image and my natural character. The chasm between my thoughts and my actions grows wider and deeper. As also, the rift between me and my fellow countrymen. My work plays no role in their daily sustenance...I fully understand that by dissociating my histrionic ability from my intrinsic ideologies, not only is a group of businessmen making money, but more importantly, my hard work helps maintain and sustain this rotten society.'*

Later, as part of the Ritwik Ghatak Memorial Lecture in 1982, nearing twenty-five years of acting, Soumitra spoke on 'Acting and Politics'. All his earlier confusions were still present though he was trying to come to terms with the idea that as an actor, a realistic representation of life would be meaningful instead of trying to find faults in the system that supported him and his family. By then, he had realized that even though an actor's art was not completely autonomous like a writer's or a director's, the actor was indeed the mouthpiece of the director.

The lament deriding acting as a vocation in 1970 was, by then, transformed into a more critical quest for the practical possibilities of depicting reality within acting. He mentioned, 'It is indeed a limitation for city actors like me to depict the realities of life in an honest way. Because, if we think carefully,

---

* Soumitra Chatterjee, *Swogoto*, Fourth Estate Publications, 1996, pp. 10-11—translated by the author.

what we know as life, the one we try to depict on screen with care, is actually the life of the same class we belong to. Beyond this class, how far do we know the lives of the people who form 80 per cent of our population? Due to the Permanent Settlement, the difference between the urban and rural, the disparity between the majority of our countrymen and the middle and upper classes who garner all the facilities of life including culture and education, which was created long back, continues to grow bigger and wider. All the centres of art, literature and culture are in the cities, mainly in Calcutta. The city-bred middle class holds the power and opportunity to practise culture. It is his mentality, his ideology that has gained prominence in our literature, poetry, music, theatre, etc. So, in the end, for an actor like me who is a product of this, my work can't reflect life's philosophy of the majority of my countrymen.'*

It will not be impertinent to point out here that in his very last film *Agantuk*, made ten years after this lecture of Soumitra, Satyajit Ray voiced a similar disillusionment, mouthed by his central character Manomohan, played by another artist of great social and political convictions—Utpal Dutt.

Soumitra's political stance and his mental disengagement with the power equation that had started since the '60s continued for decades as he slowly came to terms with this disappointment. The ruling party in the state for almost the first two decades after he debuted as an actor was the Indian National Congress led by Bidhan Chandra Roy initially, and

---

* Ibid., pp. 62-63.

later, Siddhartha Shankar Ray, apart from the Unified Front for an interim period. The entire second part of the '60s, extending well into the '70s, was marred by political unrest, worldwide student revolutions and the Naxalite movement in Bengal which soon fanned into a nationwide Maoist revolution.

At the centre, in New Delhi, it was the Indian National Congress which held sway undisputedly from Independence in 1947 till 1977 amidst widespread despair and despondency, mainly amongst the youth. Soumitra's leftist lineage made him a cynic, refusing a Padma Shree conferred on him in 1970. He repeated the same act in 1992 when he was approached once more for the award. It was only in 2004 that he accepted the more honourable Padma Bhushan and later, the highest award for cinema in the country, the Dadasaheb Phalke Award, in 2012. It will be safe to speculate that his repeated rejection of national honours, his marked and vocal leftist ideologies and his socio-political activities didn't help his chances at the National Film Awards.

***

For two films of 1967, *Chiriyakhana* and *Anthony Firingee*, superstar Uttam Kumar was conferred the best actor award at the 15th National Film Awards held the following year. It was the first time that actors and actresses were awarded for their contributions and indeed, it was a huge moment for Uttam Kumar individually and the Bengali film industry in general. However, 1967 was a very rough year for Uttam Kumar personally. His maiden venture in Hindi cinema with *Chhoti*

Si Mulaqat had been a resounding flop. More importantly, having produced the film by mortgaging his own properties, the debacle knocked Uttam hard. He suffered from a heart attack and was in dire need of money.

Shortly after this, the Bengali film industry was rocked by unrest, dissonances that had been brewing for a while. On 12 March 1968, cinema hall workers of Calcutta and Howrah went on a 100-day strike demanding a pay hike and appealing for other benefits, including special allowances. Within a month, the agitation spread to the other cities of the state and more than two hundred cinema halls came to a standstill. During that time, there was a single actors' association in Bengal, the Abhinetri Sangha, founded way back in the '50s. It was the first association in India run by actors whose purpose was to take care of the actors' causes and safeguard them. At that time, in 1968, Uttam Kumar was the president and Soumitra Chatterjee was the general secretary of Abhinetri Sangha.

On 29 May the same year, a representation of Abhinetri Sangha met the chief minister and submitted a petition supporting the hall workers along with suggesting other reforms that could uplift the industry. Unfortunately, a week after, Uttam Kumar as the president of the organization withdrew the petition. This soon started a huge turmoil within the acting fraternity of Bengali cinema and also other technicians and directors.

Soumitra, being an idealist reactionary, submitted his resignation from the post of general secretary, which was not accepted by the committee. The rift within the organization started to widen. Soon after, Uttam Kumar along with a group of actors—including Bikas Roy, Anil Chatterjee, Nirmal Kumar, Jahar Roy, Tarun Kumar, Molina Devi, Supriya Devi, Madhabi Mukherjee, Basabi Nandi and others—moved out of Abhinetri Sangha to form a parallel group called Shilpi Samsad. A sizeable chunk of actors including Subhendu Chatterjee, Biswajit, Radhamohan Bhattacharjee, Bhanu Banerjee, Anup Kumar, Basanta Chowdhury, Kali Banerjee, Utpal Dutt, Rabi Ghosh, Dilip Roy, Aparna Sen, Sharmila Tagore, Nilima Das, Lily Chakraborty, Ruma Guhathakurta stayed back under Soumitra's leadership in Abhinetri Sangha.

To the common man, the two groups appeared to be rivals even though they had camaraderie at a personal level. The famous binary of 'Uttam or Soumitra' gained more prominence from then onwards. Along with the likes of 'Mohun Bagan or East Bengal' and 'Ghati or Bangal', this has stayed on in the Bengali psyche for the last five decades.

There might have been more than what met the eye behind Uttam Kumar withdrawing support to the agitation after initially supporting it. The financial losses that he incurred due to the bungling of *Chhoti Si Mulaqat* prompted him to take loans from a few influential producers of Bengali cinema. It was assumed that those producers pressured Uttam to withdraw the petition.

Discord was looming large on other frontiers as well. An organization, primarily run by film producers, distributers and hall owners, called West Bengal Chalachchitra Sangrakshan Samiti was formed shortly before to channelize and smoothen the production-distribution of Bengali cinema. Satyajit Ray, Tapan Sinha and most of the major directors of Bengali cinema were associated with it.

However, the basic reasons for which the organization was formed soon seemed to be forgotten, salient amongst which was the movement to recycle a part of the entertainment tax back into the film industry itself. Shortly before Uttam Kumar broke away to form Shilpi Samsad, on 26 December 1968, a group of directors left the West Bengal Chalachchitra Sangrakshan Samiti as well. Led by Satyajit Ray, Tapan Sinha, Tarun Majumdar and Ajoy Kar, this group of filmmakers explained their stance on 2 January 1969 through an open letter to the press.

They reiterated their tacit and moral support towards the Samiti but not its operational inadequacies and misappropriations. Their letter didn't shy away from also showing distinct distaste as to how Shilpi Samsad was formed as a breakaway from Abhinetri Sangha and the Samiti's support and nurturing of the Samsad.

The West Bengal Chalachchitra Sangrakshan Samiti, which was playing the role of a liaison between the producer and exhibitor, didn't take it lightly. As an immediate effect, the Samiti left no stone unturned to stop the release of Satyajit Ray's *Goopi Gyne Bagha Byne*, which ran into major controversies and delays till it was finally released months later on 8 May 1969.

Eastern India Motion Pictures Association (EIMPA) was a producers' organization much like Abhinetri Sangha was one of actors. Representatives of EIMPA were members of the Samiti as well. Quite obviously, they didn't take Abhinetri Sangha's stance to support the strike of the hall workers lightly, neither could they reconcile to the fact that the biggest filmmakers were not backing the Samiti. Soon, an unofficial hand-circulated blacklist was prepared by EIMPA with the names of Soumitra, Anup

Kumar, Bhanu Banerjee among actors; Soumendu Roy, Ray's cinematographer; Ray's production manager Anil Choudhury; and filmmaker Ajit Lahiri. The list was stealthily shared with producers and directors, urging them to refrain from engaging these six in their projects.

Fortunately, ideological differences notwithstanding, the personal relations between members of the two actors' factions were not marred. Soumitra, for instance, had a deep emotional bond with Uttam. The mutual love and respect did become murky at the height of the unrest with both parties hurling abuse and derogatory remarks at each other. Yet, the two revived their cordial, respectful relations quickly. As a result, in 1969, the duo made their second film together, Salil Dutta's *Aparichito* based on Fyodor Dostoevsky's novel, *The Idiot*. Soumitra played the docile halfwit, Sujit, against the obsessively aggressive maniac Ranjan played by Uttam Kumar. Almost like a reversal of profiles from their first, *Jhinder Bandi*, *Aparichito* with an ensemble star cast was an instant hit in a year recovering from a crisis.

***

The crisis in the film industry was resolved only at an operational level. But deep within his mind, Soumitra's disillusionment with the system became indelible. It was from this unrest that he would question his own actions and conflict with his philosophies in the article 'Swogoto' in 1970. It was this confusion that lured him to write the play *Rajkumar*, adapted from Clifford Odets's *The Big Knife*. Soumitra kept intact the basic premise of the original play where an actor becomes a pawn at the hands of the producers and commits suicide unable to cope with the dilemma. But he transcreated it in the context of the unrest.

For the hero, Rajkumar, he mixed personalities and incidents encompassing both himself and Uttam Kumar. For instance, Rajkumar is shown to have marked leftist ideologies and is an active member of an actors' association. He is vocal, reactionary; his idealogy creates marital discord at home, and ultimately, his wife leaves him, thinking that by betraying the hall-workers' strike, Rajkumar has backstabbed the movement. Incidentally, Rajkumar's current conflicts with himself also happen after completing twelve years in the industry.

On the other hand, like Uttam, Rajkumar's primary conflict is the way a section of the producers keeps on piling pressure on him due to debts owed to them after the debacle of his first Hindi venture, *Yadon ki Dastan*! There was nothing random in Soumitra choosing to pen down *Rajkumar*, and mixing parts of himself and Uttam Kumar for the profile of the hero. Also, his mentor Ray's deconstruction of the hero in *Nayak* (incidentally played to immortality by Uttam Kumar) a few years ago probably influenced Soumitra.

The crisis of Ray's hero was individual and his stance was avowedly rightist (he disagrees to lend his name and support to an agitation by trade union workers led by his childhood friend Biresh), the hero in Soumitra's play is distinctly opposite in his conflict of being unable to continue his support for the strike workers. As a result, while Ray's hero goes on a self-reflective journey that ultimately reinstates the status quo, Soumitra's hero travels on a self-critical path and in the end destroys himself given his failure to destabilize the social status quo that the middle class wants to maintain at all cost.

Probably, deep down, Soumitra's angst against the system was so deep-rooted that he realized that one article in a magazine was not enough to vent his frustration and anger. *Rajkumar* was dedicated to Bengali cinema's workers and technicians; it was first published in Soumitra-edited *Ekshan* in 1974 and as a book in 1975 from Subarnarekha Publications. A year before that, on 4 December 1973, Soumitra first staged this play in Rabindra Sadan as part of a theatre festival organized by Abhinetri Sangha. Only a decade later, when Soumitra had already established himself as a viable theatre personality as well with *Naam Jiban*, did he regularly stage *Rajkumar* on the commercial stage at the Kashi Biswanath Mancha in North Calcutta.

Both Shilpi Samsad and Abhinetri Sangha continued to function for years, with the mission to uplift the conditions of lowly paid technicians. While Shilpi Samsad produced films including *Banpalashir Padabali* directed by Uttam Kumar, Abhinetri Sangha organized theatre festivals to raise money. The first theatre festival spanned four shows on 4, 5, 7 and 10 December 1973 with the staging of *Rajkumar*, *Hathat Nabab*, *Bidehi* and *Crushbiddho Cuba*. In the last play, directed by Utpal Dutt, Soumitra played a minor role.

Not only *Rajkumar*, Soumitra also adapted (from Henrik Ibsen's *Ghosts*), directed and acted in the main role of *Bidehi*. Two years later, in February 1976, Abhinetri Sangha organized its second theatre festival over four nights. Apart from *Bidehi* and *Rajkumar*, the two other plays this time were Saratchandra Chatterjee's *Grihadaha* and *20se June*. Soumitra didn't act in *Grihadaha* but was the main character in the other three—of which *20se June* was directed by noted theatre and cinema actor, Jnanesh Mukherjee.

Both theatre festivals were Soumitra's idea, and he had a very clear-cut thought process behind them. Even earlier since its inception in the early '50s, Abhinetri Sangha had staged a few plays for relief purposes. Soumitra himself acted in some of them under others' direction; such as Rabindranath Tagore's *Sesh Raksha* and *Muktir Upay*, both directed by Anup Kumar. While the money-raising objective of these shows was always met, Soumitra was critical about the acting and production standards of these one-off shows. To him, a production from an actors' association comprising so many great actors could never afford to be one of low standards.

His aim behind the two festivals, hence, was to cater to healthy entertainment for the common audience with a good production quality and superior acting. The commercial and aesthetic success of the two theatre festivals and critical appreciation for *Bidehi* and *Rajkumar* bolstered Soumitra's belief to take to theatre seriously.

The decision to turn to his first love—theatre—not as one-off shows as part of Abhinetri Sangha festivals, but on a regular, frequent basis, was based on a couple of related realizations. First and foremost, as he matured in the industry, his growing discontent with his work awakened him to the reality that most of the roles he would get would be mindless. To preserve his sanctity and ideological beliefs, Soumitra needed a parallel track to keep himself grounded. Theatre gave him that platform where he would write the roles he wished to do himself.

His growing dissatisfaction with being just a representative of someone else's vision, be it a writer or a director, marginalized his creative aspirations in cinema. In theatre, he started carving a niche for himself by being the writer, director and actor all rolled in one, something he couldn't do in cinema. After a decade-long journey as an actor and an editor of a magazine, Soumitra's creative hunger egged him on to take up more artistically gratifying responsibilities.

Secondly, in the '70s, he performed almost the same number of roles as he had done in the previous decade but this time, Satyajit Ray cast him four times, Ajoy Kar thrice and Tarun Majumdar once. The likes of Mrinal Sen and Tapan Sinha had moved on to younger heroes. Sen introduced Ranjit Mallik in *Interview* (1970) and then Mithun Chakraborty in *Mrigaya* (1976) and cast Dhritiman Chaterjee in *Padatik* in 1973. Tapan Sinha, on the other hand, relied on Swarup Dutta in *Ekhoni* (1971), Debraj Ray in *Raja* (1975) and Dipankar Dey in *Ek Je Chhilo Desh* (1977). Even Soumitra's mentor Satyajit Ray looked at three younger actors to portray the three faces of the city youth in his Calcutta Trilogy of the '70s.

With his intelligent analysis, Soumitra comprehended that as he wouldn't be getting younger every passing year, chances of enacting central characters in the films of better directors would diminish. Unlike the '60s, when he was the automatic choice of the thinking director which defined and shaped him as an actor extraordinaire, it was the mainstream melodramas of the '70s that would keep his pot boiling.

After writing *Rajkumar*, Soumitra wrote *Brihannala* adapted from Sean O'Casey's *The Shadow of a Gunman*. Written in 1978 but set in 1970, the protagonist of this play is a poet. Looking back, for this play, the writer Soumitra brought up the fear and unrest of 1970—both by the armed police and also the radical extremists. More than anything else, many a contemporary cultural outpouring of the turbulence made the non-committal, compromising middle class face the mirror. And that is why when, at the very end, Minu, a slum dweller with no apparent relation with the armed movement, dies in a police firing, the protagonist of the play, poet Dhiren, turns to the audience with a monologue—'Till the time you live, the stain of Minu's blood will taint your hands. Will you again write poetry with those hands?…Minu is dead. It is bad without a doubt. But even worse is that so many like us, scared, cowardly, opportunist will remain alive. Shame, Dhiren, Shame.'*

There is no mistaking that like Rajkumar, Soumitra poured all his dilemma into Dhiren and used the profile to whip himself in an attempt to redeem his own battered, humane soul.

On 21 December 1978, Soumitra launched *Naam Jiban* in Kashi Biswanath Mancha. The play was adapted from Errol John's *Moon on a Rainbow Shawl*. Soumitra was clear right from the beginning that he would be involved in commercial Bengali theatre of North Calcutta, the one in which he first shared the stage with his mentor, Sisir Kumar Bhaduri. The

---

* Soumitra Chatterjee, 'Brihannala', *Natak Samagra Vol 1*, Ananda Publishers Private Ltd, 2019 (Second Edition), p. 203—translated by the author.

other theatre, which is popularly known as the Group Theatre, was apparently the more intellectual one.

It is quite remarkable to note that most of the practitioners of Group Theatre had leftist ideologies and they believed that theatre as an art should have high intellectual quotient; theatre needed to be uncompromising as opposed to cinema being a populist art form. In achieving this, like many so-called 'art' films, the Group Theatre slowly dissociated itself from the general audience, and the economy of Bengali theatre dried up. The commercial space, the one that had flourished in Bengal since the days of Girish Ghosh till Sisir Kumar Bhaduri, which was more commonly known in Bengali as 'Sadharon Rongaloy', adopted a crude, inane entertaining genre in the 1960s.

At this juncture, for Soumitra—with his leftist stance—to not join the Group Theatre bandwagon was startling to say the least. He was steadfast in his belief that the audience abandoned commercial theatre because they were served rank bad material in the name of entertainment. It was the same problem he had in accepting the initial below-standard productions of Abhinetri Sangha.

Soumitra in a sense revived the status of commercial Bengali theatre almost single-handedly. And he did so with a clarity of thought, superlative acting performances and elaborate sets. His experience with Satyajit Ray influenced him to look for details and also to be fastidious to achieve authenticity. For example, for the earlier play *Bidehi*, for a portrait of the absent Captain Alving, Soumitra researched different Scandinavian military dresses of that time and had a portrait drawn accordingly—to be showcased on the set just as a prop.

In addition, Soumitra's own naturalistic cinema acting evolved a pattern of understated theatre acting hitherto unknown, both on commercial stage and in Group Theatre. Most of his plays were successful hits with a few hundred shows in each, and mostly house-full. As a theatre personality, his greatest contribution was to bring the general Bengali audience back to the commercial stage.

In the plays he wrote, he was careful to have meaty roles for himself, one of the primary reasons he drifted to theatre. The theatre-director Soumitra brought the film star to his theatre, a definite reason why *Naam Jiban* was initially a curiosity for all. But soon, Soumitra's theatre survived on its own and flourished beyond his cinema star's image. To his credit, Soumitra included his political ideology in the plays he chose, the adaptations he made and also in the dialogues the characters delivered. He never went overboard with propagandist slogans, yet in theatre after theatre, even in the apparently comic *Ghatak Biday*, he—as the playwright—shone as a progressive, liberal human being.

***

The '70s saw Uttam Kumar beginning to take to character roles, leaving aside romantic leads. The mental turmoil he had undergone had started taking a toll on his physique as well by leaving a mark on his appearance. He looked bloated, tired and unhappy. To make matters worse, Uttam Kumar continued to try out his luck in a few Hindi films and was never at ease in any of them.

The general quality of Bengali films too started to slide in the '70s. The angst of the Bengali youth, the politically tumultuous Naxal movement, needed a new crop of young filmmakers to address the reality of the times. Unfortunately, apart from the likes of Ray, Sinha and Sen, most of the other directors looked away from contemporary reality and still relied on the typical mainstream melodrama. While in Hindi cinema, the mantle changed from romance (Rajesh Khanna) to angst (Amitabh Bachchan), Bengali cinema failed to mature in content and expression.

While on one hand Uttam's Bengali films of the era represented crass melodrama, a much younger Soumitra started spreading his wings towards a well-thought-out blend of mainstream and serious films. As a professional actor, Soumitra was always open to all sorts of films. But the interesting aspect to note here is that in the '60s, his acting technique had a poetic ambivalence, a minimalistic expressive mode and a very organic style. As the films became less subtle in the '70s and as the superstar Uttam started to seem—in some of the films at least—less super, Soumitra adopted an acting style that was more expressive, at times loud.

The poetic fervour of the young Apu or a sprightly Amal or even the ruffian in *Teen Bhuvaner Paare* was soon lost in an over-the-top acting smartness that was to an extent a mark of most of the superheroes of Indian cinema. As Uttam Kumar started a journey towards character roles before his untimely death, and as newer actors started snatching younger roles in the films of serious directors, Soumitra had no other option but to change his profile to remain relevant.

Triumph and Turmoil

Uttam Kumar with Soumitra Chatterjee during the shooting of *Jadi Jantem* in 1974
(Photo Credit: Sukumar Roy)

As an intimate reader of the situation, Soumitra went for an image makeover and changed his looks slightly, keeping longer hair, shifting the parting of his hair from the middle to a side and growing longer and prominent sideburns. In his dress, in films and also in public appearances, he moved away from the earlier simple kurta and dhoti to flashier, designer shirts and trousers. The change in his appearance is so marked that most of his profile pictures in the films of the '60s look vividly different from the '70s. Film stars, mostly heroes, seldom change their looks and hairstyles once they become popular—the likes of Uttam Kumar, Dilip Kumar or Amitabh Bachchan preserved their own as they struggled with a receding hairline.

It is no wonder then that in 1982, in the Ritwik Ghatak Memorial Lecture, he disparaged himself and raised the question about an actor's lack of identity with the masses his films hoped to entertain. The thirst for identification however was quenched partially in Ray's *Ashani Sanket* (The Distant Thunder) in 1973. This was Soumitra's eighth feature film out of fourteen with Satyajit Ray. To play Gangacharan, the village Brahmin priest, Soumitra insisted that he would accompany Ray for the location recce. Soumitra took notes about how the villagers speak, sit, use their hands and fiddle with 'poite' (sacred thread worn by Brahmin males), their walking postures including the angle of feet with the toes pointing outside.

It was he who finalized the dialect in which Gangacharan would speak and chose the glasses that the character would wear. His rapport with Ray was so deep that Ray didn't object to these suggestions. The detailed notes in his diary during the recce were later published in magazines and can be a very important source of information for budding actors about how to prepare oneself for a difficult role. It is to be noted that Soumitra's upbringing in Krishnanagar in the 1940s helped him identify with the setting of *Ashani Sanket*.

There were villages on the other side of Jalangi river and in his childhood, Soumitra and a couple of his friends would at times roam there aimlessly. These memories along with the shocking one of the Bengal Famine on which *Ashani Sanket* was based enabled Soumitra's total immersion in the character and in the narrative of the film.

Ashani Sanket went on to win the Golden Bear for the Best Film at the 23rd edition of the Berlin Film Festival. It remained the only one from Ray's repertoire to win the highest award at Berlin, and till 2021, the only Indian film to win the award. It was rumoured that Soumitra's name was proposed and probably unanimously agreed upon by the juries for the Best Actor award. However, in Berlin, there was a convention that two major awards were not given to the same film. This put the juries in a big fix.

They were gracious enough to decide that none of the actors of the other films in competition were worthy of the award in lieu of Soumitra. Hence, that year, Berlin Film Festival didn't bestow the Best Actor award to any international actor! This loss, which Soumitra came to know of much later from British film critic Derek Malcolm, is paramount in the context of acting in Indian cinema. The award would have been the

Satyajit Ray directing Soumitra and Babita in *Ashani Sanket*
(Photo Credit: Sukumar Roy)

first for an Indian actor in one of the most prestigious film festivals of the world.

A year after playing a Brahmin priest of rural Bengal set in the 1940s in *Ashani Sanket*, Ray transported Soumitra to contemporary Calcutta of the mid-'70s as the dashing detective Feluda. Feluda is a modern detective, a Bengali Sherlock Holmes but directed at adolescents, teenagers and young adults. The first Feluda story, *Feludar Goendagiri*, came out in 1966 in *Sandesh*, the children's literary magazine edited by Satyajit Ray. The success of *Feludar Goendagiri* led Ray to write the adventures of Feluda and his associates regularly.

Most interestingly, and hence appealing to the teenagers of the '70s, Ray based his stories in different locations, from Lucknow and Haridwar to Gangtok, from Rajasthan to Shimla or from Aurangabad to Benares. This thriller-cum-travelogue soon caught the imagination of young minds and Feluda became a rage. It was probably a matter of time before Ray made a film on Feluda after the remarkable success of *Goopi Gyne Bagha Byne* based on a children's novel by Ray's grandfather, Upendra Kishore Raychoudhuri.

Ray made two Feluda films—*Sonar Kella* in 1974, locating the thriller in Rajasthan, and then *Joy Baba Felunath* five years later in 1979 in Benares. Soumitra always felt that Ray had imparted a lot of himself in the character of Felu, mainly the ability to keep an open mind about new things and more importantly, assimilating information into knowledge.

In realizing Ray's vision of Feluda, Soumitra kept in mind that the detective was a thinking person and unlike most Western detectives, he was less physical and more of an intellectual. Yet, he was markedly different from an average Bengali of the time. In expressing the mental toughness of Feluda, his intelligence, his resolve to not merely unearth a crime but to steadfastly stand for justice and against all wrongs, Soumitra used his eyes to great effect, differently from his other characterizations. He observed the different forms of Indian classical dance, mainly Kathakali, and picked up a few gestures using the eyes.

Feluda went on to become a character, like Apu, synonymous with Soumitra. Both Feluda films became instant hits with young minds. Soumitra was particularly happy to play the role because it was the first time that he was acting in a profile that would cater to his own teenage children.

***

Along with acting in cinema and apart from writing, directing and acting in theatre, the other diversification of Soumitra's creative personality which found expression at this time was poetry. From his grandfather and father, Soumitra had inherited the ability to recite poems from a very young age. While his father would recite poetry at competitions and win awards, Soumitra's mother would recite Tagore's verses to put her children to sleep. Right from his school days, Soumitra used to get awarded for his recitation. He continued reciting poems without fail in his college days and later in many of his films as well.

However, the change from a reciter reading poems to his friends or informal audiences out of his own love for the medium to a seasoned professional elocutionist happened primarily when Abhinetri Sangha regularly organized shows to raise funds. Abhinetri Sangha's programmes and theatre festivals were not for any financial rewards for the participants; all who took part in them did so without any fee and due to their love and support for the cause.

The fiasco with the Sangrakshan Samiti that had resulted in an embargo on him and others made Soumitra rethink his stance as primarily a cinema actor. He realized that the industry and his future were both uncertain. Moving to Bombay was not an option either. He had witnessed the fate of Uttam Kumar.

Sharmila Tagore, his co-star in his first two films, had been successful in Hindi films by then. As was his friend Biswajit. But Biswajit and Tagore did not have much acclaim and fame to leave behind in Calcutta in the Bengali film industry when they made their way to Bombay. Hence, trying their luck in Hindi films was a low risk for both. For Soumitra, the stakes were way too high in case he, like Uttam, couldn't shed off the 'Bengali' image in a Hindi-language industry. That image was wrapped all around him and defined him in the minds of the average Bengali.

Elocution is a practice in Bengali culture, a form of performative art which is prevalent enough. Elocution by individuals, a collective, oral theatres—all of them have quite a significant number of takers even now. Cinema and theatre actors have always been regular voices in elocutions though there has been a constant stream of practitioners from other fields too. Like his acting in cinema and theatre, Soumitra introduced a non-theatrical style of poetry reading. He indulged in voice modulations when necessary but overall, it was marked by a naturalistic rendition laced with necessary inflections to make the experience worthwhile, a trait that highlighted his acting career for six decades.

In parallel to reading poetry of his favourite poets, like Tagore, Jibanananda Das, Samar Sen and Subhas Mukhopadhyay, Soumitra was fond of presenting poems of contemporary poets as well, including those of his friends, Shakti Chatterjee and Sunil Ganguly. Unless compelled, Soumitra seldom recited his own poems in public functions and programmes.

Soumitra had started writing poems at a young age, when the first feelings of adolescent love had engulfed him. His initial poems were addressed to Deepa. But soon, his relationship with nature and a critical look at the society around him started appearing in his poetry. When he was an announcer in All India Radio, Soumitra was down with chickenpox for almost a month. He was unmarried then but was seeing Deepa quite regularly. He had a habit of gifting books to Deepa on her birthday till then.

That year, being bedridden, Soumitra didn't get a chance to go out of his home to buy a book. Instead, he translated the entire *Rubáiyát of Omar Khayyám* by Edward Fitzgerald into Bengali and presented it to her. Since then, Soumitra always presented poems on his wife's birthday and later to his children and then his grandchildren on their birthdays. Poulami being a professional dancer, it was quite natural that the connotation of dance resurfaced prominently in his poems to her. On the other hand, since Sougata was born in the Bengali month of 'Ashwin', that reference recurred in poems for him.

Soumitra always felt embarrassed about his initial poems but his quantum leap in terms of experience and exposure came when he graduated to college and started being part of Calcutta life. That young age of exploration coupled with the experience of the reality of a big city endowed Soumitra with a vision and shaped his creative sensitivities. His senior in college, Gourmohan Mukherjee, instilled the habit of regular writing. Gourmohan gave another jewel of an advice to Soumitra—to forget the most recent writing as quickly as possible so that the next poem could be welcomed.

Being friends with established poets like Shakti and Sunil helped Soumitra's poetic skills but it also made him reluctant to bring out a book of his own poems. Shakti insisted to Soumitra, much like Gourmohan, that unless a set of poems was published as a book, a new form of writing would be difficult to embrace. It was Shakti who eventually brought the publishers of Annapurna Publishing to Soumitra, reassuring him that he was working just as a liaison since the publishers had approached him to introduce them to Soumitra.

Eventually, the first collection of Soumitra's poetry anthology *Jalapropater Dhare Danrabo Bole* (To Stand Beside the Waterfall) was published in 1975, the same year when *Rajkumar* was published in book format by Subarnarekha with a cover design by Satyajit Ray.

Since then, Soumitra started bringing out poetry anthologies with regular frequency. He has nineteen published collections including a 'Selected Volume'. Poetry gave him a freedom of expression that his acting career couldn't provide him with. He voiced his opinions, his pains, his frustrations and fear in his theatre with equal panache but poetry, as with any poet, was always more intimate and personal. More importantly, in poetry, Soumitra was absolutely uninhibited. It was a shelter from the pressures and uncertainties in both his personal and professional life.

FIVE

Consolidating the Transition

Throughout the first two decades of his acting, Soumitra averaged three to four films a year while Uttam Kumar roughly doubled that number. The financial state of the Bengali film industry was so poor that the number of films produced yearly and the revenue they generated were unimaginably low for a fraternity that garnered so much recognition in terms of its merit—nationally and internationally. Soumitra once told me that at his peak, in the late '60s or maybe early '70s, he would be paid a fee of Rs 70-80,000 per film, second only to Uttam Kumar and Suchitra Sen, both of whom would cross the six-digit mark. During that time, a lower-ranked Hindi film star would happily take home an amount quite a few times more.

Hence, it was imperative for Soumitra, and probably Uttam as well, to succumb to popular demands which slowly but surely started drifting towards inane melodrama and blunt copying of Hindi films.

Soumitra had a bigger demon to fight. Not only was he disgruntled with a majority of the roles he was offered since the mid-'70s, but he was also disillusioned with the entire system of selling his hard work that sustained the ills of the society in terms of distribution of wealth. As Uttam Kumar started reframing his image as the misunderstood and self-forgetful elder brother, modelling himself slightly on the style of Chhabi Biswas, but more than that playing the role of conscience, Soumitra was more and more playing the confused reality of the time. In doing so, he was often paired up with the neo-liberal woman representative in Aparna Sen.

If Uttam had Suchitra Sen in the '50s, Soumitra flourished with Aparna in the '70s, commercially. Soumitra's pairing with Sharmila Tagore didn't take off after the initial prospect with Tagore leaving Calcutta for Bombay, while his on-screen chemistry with Madhabi Mukherjee was more for the elite than the masses. Aparna Sen first debuted in 1961 in Satyajit Ray's *Samapti* (the third part of *Teen Kanya*) as a teenage girl opposite Soumitra. She followed it up with Mrinal Sen's *Akash Kusum* and Nityananda Datta's *Baksho Badal*, both in 1965 and both with Soumitra in the lead.

As the feminist fervour started sweeping Indian shores, Aparna Sen of the '70s was coming up steadily as the thinking woman on the Bengali screen and indeed a daring one. Often, she revelled in roles that were an anathema for the conservative 'domesticated' woman, as the smuggler's aide or the fallen socialite, in films like *Aparichito* (opposite both Uttam Kumar and Soumitra), *Ekhane Pinjar* (opposite Uttam Kumar) or *Padma Golap* (opposite Soumitra). Sensuous but not overtly sexy, the image perfected a few years later in Hindi films by Zeenat Aman and Parveen Babi, Aparna was carving out a new prima donna image for herself in Bengali cinema.

Soumitra Chatterjee with Aparna Sen in Mrinal Sen's *Akash Kusum*
(Photo Credit: From the private collection of the Mrinal Sen family)

Indeed, the hero opposite her also had to be a product of outward chaos, an amalgamation of street violence, educated loafer with a somewhat confused, bridled sexuality. With Uttam Kumar visibly past his age, it was Soumitra and a few other actors—including Swarup Dutta, Subhendu Chatterjee and Samit Bhanja—who were trying to bring this character alive on screen.

As the definition and perspective of the modern, contemporary youth was changing in social life, Bengali commercial cinema unfortunately mistook the chaos around for clamour. On one hand, there were films that vehemently tried to depict an earlier socio-political and familial reality. And, on the other, there were films which apparently seemed to reflect the contemporary times albeit superficially, only in external markers like the dress and grooming styles of the heroes and heroines.

The introspection and vision to analyse the angst and shifts were absent, films and characters were developed alien to both their makers and the audience. In this commotion, Soumitra was finding it even more difficult to sustain. Though younger to Uttam Kumar, age was not on his side either. Newer heroes were chosen both in arthouse films as well as commercial ones. When Soumitra stepped into commercial theatre with *Naam Jiban* in 1978, he did so professionally with a vision to continue for a longer stint.

***

Theatre became Soumitra's breathing space after acting in a series of mindless melodramas as a professional actor. Along with that, quite consciously, from the late '70s, he started taking up unconventional

Soumitra Chatterjee as Aghor in *Sansar Simante*
(Photo Credit: Sukumar Roy)

character roles, remarkable choices for most popular heroes of the screen. This is how he landed up playing the role of a petty thief Aghor in Tarun Majumdar's *Sansar Simante* in 1975.

Two filmmakers of repute, Ritwik Ghatak and Rajen Tarafdar, wanted to make this film earlier about the love and loss between a prostitute and a thief. But they couldn't do so and finally, it was made by Majumdar with Tarafdar's screenplay. It was rumoured that the role was initially offered to Uttam Kumar, who declined, considering the debased image of the character.

Samit Bhanja was a regular in Tarun Majumdar's films at that time but he didn't wish to shed his athletic looks either. Premendra Mitra's short story was already Soumitra's favourite. When the role was offered to him, he grabbed it with both hands. Interestingly enough, Soumitra was strengthening his on-screen chemistry with Aparna Sen in parallel with two more films in that very year. If *Chhutir Fande* was an out-and-out romantic comedy, buoyed by the success of *Basanta Bilap* with the same star couple in the lead a couple of seasons back, *Nishimrigaya* was a thriller of sorts, where Soumitra played the role of a police officer hunting down a smuggling assistant played by Sen.

Soumitra strived continuously to diversify his scope and spectrum. In the very next year, in 1976, he acted in *Sudur Niharika*, the only one in his career in which he acted in three roles. Yet, the shift away from traditional literary sources, which were the strong backbone of mainstream Bengali cinema in the '50s and '60s, cost the local film industry quite dearly. Most of these cinematic adventures were hence freaky misadventures at best, and Soumitra's struggle to remain afloat continued. He was carving his path in theatre, immersing himself in poetry and at the same time consciously looking to break the romantic image on screen and opening up to explorations with his physical self.

Many heroes, including Uttam Kumar, had advised Soumitra not to experiment with his looks as he did in *Samapti*, *Abhijan*, *Ashani Sanket* and surely in *Sansar Simante*. They feared that the box-office won't approve of a romantic hero veering away from his acceptedly gifted looks and charm. Soumitra would never reconcile himself with this line of thought. To defy all odds, he entered professional theatre at an age when he was the second-most popular hero of Bengali cinema.

Indeed, his stardom brought in a stream of audience to his theatre in the initial days. However, the flow never ebbed, because of the quality of experience he brought in his theatre. To his credit, Soumitra never thought that his silver-screen glory would be compromised if audiences would get to watch him in person for three days a week without fail.

Just as he went off the beaten track to embrace theatre as one of the most distinguished traits of his creative will, so he did when he moved to character roles which looked and breathed differently from the commercial hero ones. As a result, the audience had the opportunity to see him as Udayan Pandit of Satyajit Ray's *Hirak Rajar Deshe* in 1980, extending to *Agradani* in 1983 and then to Tapan Sinha's *Atanka* or Saroj De's *Kony* in 1986.

***

This wilful transition to act the roles of characters either different from his own socio-economic class or older than him in age at that time marks Soumitra's skilful choice as an actor more than a hero. It can be reasoned that if in the '60s, Soumitra strengthened his mettle in cinema, and the '70s marks his drifting away to other art forms, it was the '80s which is his period of transition as a cinema actor. And his rediscovery of his cinematic career as well.

In the '60s, it was the feminine aspects of Soumitra's physical charm that lent poetic licence to his self-absorbed non-acting style. It was this very quality which made Aparna's mother attribute godly qualities to a young Apu in *Apur Sansar*. The same attribute made Amulya in *Samapti* as naïve as his newly wed bride. With the same compassionate affection, Charu looked at Amal in *Charulata* or Archana tore off Sukhendu's dress in *Saat Paake Bandha*.

Even in *Akash Kusum*, irrespective of Ajoy's fraudulent behaviour, it was his delicate tenderness which leaves the audience rooting for him. Almost throughout the '60s, with a few exceptions like *Abhijan* or *Jhinder Bandi*, Soumitra instilled a delicate, tender grace in the body of the hero. No mistaking it, Soumitra's sex appeal as a hero in the '60s was different from Uttam Kumar's more masculine mien. If Uttam Kumar was the winner, Soumitra more often than not excelled in being the defeated other in the films of the '60s.

In a majority of the films in which they acted together, apart from *Jhinder Bandi*, the two heroes of Bengali cinema complemented each other in style and characterization in the likes of *Aparichito*, *Stree*, *Devdas* and *Jadi Jantem*. Uttam was the more confident go-getter. Soumitra, the more sublime, more subtle, romantic loser.

With the '70s, Soumitra's change in physical appearance added a shade of masculinity to his image. However, in the '80s, he extended this experimentation further. Two films stand out in this milieu—Tapan Sinha's *Atanka* and Saroj De's *Kony*. The image of a defeated romantic youth now transcended to a middle-class, educated Bengali who was ready to take on the world at large. From the '70s, Tapan Sinha, like Satyajit Ray, was moving away from depicting classics on screen. Both Mrinal Sen and Satyajit Ray had their own Calcutta Trilogies reflecting the angst and anger of the youth in the early '70s as a direct reflection of the confused state of affairs.

Sinha also had his own, less celebrated, urban trilogy of sorts in *Aponjan* (1968), *Ekhone* (1971) and *Raja* (1975). Unlike Sen, who was known for his pronounced communist traits, or Ray who was mostly ambivalent in terms of his preferences, Sinha left no stone unturned to voice his resentment of the communist rule in Bengal and communism in general. In 1982, he made *Adalat o Ekti Meye* on the vilification of the petty middle-class ego and sentiments when a young girl is gangraped on a sea beach. Sinha was vocal against the rampant lumpenization of the youth which was on the rise at that time. Many of these local goons were openly sheltered by the influential political leaders.

A shocking film, it was surely one of the rarest ones of the time to portray a ghastly incident with such bold political undertones. Sinha followed *Adalat o Ekti Meye* up with *Atanka*, where a retired schoolteacher finds himself cornered by thugs after he witnesses a political murder in the locality. He is rounded up, petrified, his son is brutally abused and daughter made a victim of acid attack. Sinha always maintained that he picked the incidents from newspapers and even though they seemed grim and unreal, they were actually happening.

Atanka was a bigger success than *Adalat o Ekti Meye*. Mostly because from 1982 to 1986, from the first five years of the communist rule to the near completion of the next, things worsened in Bengal and Calcutta. Hence, the absolute failure of the police forces and the hapless victimization of the middle class were better realized by the audience. Secondly, by making a retired old teacher a victim, Sinha appealed to a wider cross-section of the audience. But to top it all, it was Soumitra's breathtaking performance which sealed the film and makes it a memorable outing even now.

For this, Soumitra sported a marked old look with a special denture to break his natural graceful profile. It was a pity that the best actor award at the 34th National Film Awards didn't come Soumitra's way. It went to Charu Hasan for an immensely moving yet thoroughly controlled portrayal of an individual's anguish and sufferings, waiting for justice, in Girish Kasaravalli's equally evocative *Tabarane Katha*. The extremely nuanced and sensitive film went on to win the best film award that year as well.

In *Atanka*, the old teacher was a representative of the quintessential Bengali 'bhadralok'—the sufferer who finally musters courage to rise from the ashes, metaphorically. In *Kony*, released in the same year, Soumitra played the role of a swimming coach Khidda who could inspire Kanakchampa Pal aka Kony, a slumdweller, to compete with more privileged athletes and win laurels for herself and later, her state. For the role of Khidda as well, Soumitra altered his natural good looks, wore a nicely cropped wig, sported a pair of high-power glasses and applied make-up to tone down his natural skin glow.

Inspired by Moti Nandi's eponymous novel, it was Soumitra himself who drew a figure of Khidda to discuss with the director what the trainer should look like. Khidda remains, till date, one of Soumitra's oft-referred roles. Khidda's rousing cry, 'Fight, Kony, fight', has become an embodiment of an unvanquished spirit to live and excel in the Bengali mass culture. Soumitra himself admitted that in times of depression and agony, Khidda's unyielding attitude helped him ride the abyss. Though released on 3 January 1986, *Kony* was made earlier and it won the National Film Award for Best Popular Film Providing Wholesome Entertainment at the 32nd National Film Awards. Unfortunately for Soumitra, he lost out again, this time to Naseeruddin Shah's stellar performance in Goutam Ghosh's *Paar*.

At the same 32nd National Film Awards, the best supporting actor award went to Victor Banerjee for Nikhilesh in Satyajit Ray's *Ghare Baire*. *Ghare Baire* was a film Ray had been planning to make even before *Pather Panchali*. In their initial days of collaboration, Ray would tell Soumitra that he was considering him to play Nikhilesh. Later, he would mention that Soumitra would fit better as Sandip, the sly yet sophisticated villain opposite Nikhilesh. Ray joked that Soumitra would fit both characters with ease. Depending on finding an actor who would be suitable for any of the two roles, the other would go to Soumitra.

However, much before the shooting of the film actually started in December 1982, Ray finalized Soumitra to play Sandip. He had two reasons for this decision. First, for Bimala to fall in love with Sandip in spite of a morally upright and physically attractive husband Nikhilesh, Sandip needed to be an equally charismatic person. Soumitra with his romantic on-screen image provided the necessary swagger to sweep Bimala off her feet.

Secondly, in the screenplay, there were lengthy dialogues and Ray understood that apart from Soumitra, there weren't many in Bengali cinema who had the clarity of diction to deliver the lines with the flair that they needed. Soumitra's Sandip remains one of his best performances and arguably second only to *Jhinder Bandi* in a negative role.

***

Even though Soumitra's third completed film with Tapan Sinha happened in 1986 with *Atanka*, it was in 1983 that Soumitra returned to Sinha's team after a hiatus of two decades. The film, named *Abhimanyu*, with Soumitra and Madhabi Mukherjee in the lead roles, was also the couple's first after fifteen years. Unfortunately, shooting of the film ran into a few difficulties and it was finally stalled. Seven years later, Sinha directed its Hindi version as *Ek Doctor Ki Maut*, which fetched him a National Award for best direction and Pankaj Kapur, the central character, a special jury award.

Working with Soumitra after two decades made Sinha realize how much the actor had matured over the years and since then, Soumitra remained almost a regular in the films Sinha made till his last. His immediate next two Bengali ventures after *Atanka* were *Antardhan* in 1992 and *Wheel Chair* in 1994. With these films, Soumitra nurtured a new profile of the elderly and the aged in Bengali cinema. For the next three decades, he perfected that image with occasional variations.

In his youth, he didn't follow any particular actor to shape his own acting style. Sisir Bhaduri instilled a philosophy, a vision and a belief in a young Soumitra that art ends when imitation starts. Fortunately for Bengali cinema, when Soumitra matured to play the aged and the old, he never wished to follow the models available in Chhabi Biswas, Kamal Mitra, Pahari Sanyal and a few others.

While Soumitra was experimenting with his looks and roles in cinema, in parallel, he was exploring his literary self in his verses. His second book of poems, *Byaktigoto Nakshatramala* (A Personal Bead of Stars), was published in 1976, the third, *Sabdara Amaar Bagane* (The Words in My Garden), in 1981 and then, *Porey Achhe Chandaner Chita* (There Lies the Sandal Pyre) in 1983. The covers of these first four anthologies were designed and illustrated by none other than Soumitra's mentor and guide, Satyajit Ray.

The year 1986 marks a few important milestones for Soumitra. On 30 May that year, with the release of *Shyam Shaheb* and *Urbashi*, he completed a century of released films. A couple of months prior to that, Soumitra left his rented apartment at 3 Lake Temple Road (which was previously inhabited by Satyajit Ray; Ray himself had arranged for Soumitra to move in once he left) and moved into his two-storeyed bungalow at Golf Green. It remained his abode till the end, a mark of his aesthetic tastes laced with minimalistic qualities. It was in 1986 that Soumitra first ventured into film direction when he made *Stree ka Patra*, a Hindi adaptation of Rabindranath Tagore's 'Stree-r Patra'. The telefilm was broadcast on Doordarshan's national transmission to mark the 125th birth anniversary of the bard.

***

Soumitra never ventured to Bombay (Mumbai now) to try his luck in Hindi cinema. He feared that his freedom to pursue a lot of things in Calcutta then—including his theatre, his writings and editing *Ekshan*—would be curbed. He declined Hrishikesh Mukherjee's offer to play Dr Bhaskar Banerjee in the 1971 blockbuster *Anand* opposite superstar Rajesh Khanna. The role went to Amitabh Bachchan, who excelled in a controlled and subdued performance, fetching him a *Filmfare* award and public recognition for the first time.

A few years later, Soumitra initially got interested but finally didn't act in Shyam Benegal's *Kalyug*. It was during the time when he directed *Stree ka Patra* that Soumitra acted in two other Hindi telefilms—*Nirpuama* (based on Tagore's 'Dena Paona') and *Dadaji* (based on Tagore's 'Thakurda'). However, his first foray to act in a Hindi-language film, again a telefilm, happened in 1985, when he acted in Arundhati Devi's *Gokul*. Soumitra went on to act in a few other Hindi telefilms including *Ahankar* by Raja Mitra based on Ramapada Choudhury's novel *Chhad*. Incidentally, twenty years later,

Soumitra acted in Anik Dutta's Bengali feature *Borunbabur Bondhu* based on the same story and in the same role.

Apart from directing *Stree ka Patra*, Soumitra hadn't taken to film direction ever. He always maintained that in those days, in the '70s and '80s, when he could have directed films, it would have occupied him full-time for quite a few months. Being a professional actor of a marginalized film industry in terms of commerce, he couldn't afford that. Also, he believed that to be a serious filmmaker, he should have started to pick up the nuances of the craft earlier. As an observant actor at the top of his craft, he was better placed than any newcomer to the trade.

But Soumitra's biggest strength had always been his sharp judgement about his own capabilities. This held him in good stead and saved him from momentous and shattering failures. However, if his hunger for scripting his vision and philosophies was satiated by his writing and adapting plays, directing them quenched his creative yearnings as a theatre-maker. In accordance with the demands and expectations of the commercial theatre, where he started to stage his plays, the set designs were elaborate. But instead of being just a façade, the director in Soumitra used its minutest details to make the viewing experience more wholesome.

In Satyajit Ray's cinema, the acting style involved most of the non-actors engaged in trivial businesses along with dialogue deliveries to complement the dialogue with their actions. This freed them of tension and made their acting natural and realistic. Soumitra introduced to his theatre his own experience and expertise in this sort of cinematic non-acting. That is why in his very first play, *Naam Jiban*, the stage of a lower-middle-class household 'acted' as well. The actors would do mundane jobs, regular household chores using the length and breadth of the stage.

Biswa, the protagonist played by Soumitra, for instance, was seen cleaning and repairing his cycle on stage and then pedalling it across as an extremely realistic performance within the aegis of commercial theatre. In his next, *Rajkumar*, the audience would find Rajkumar, a film star, watching a clip of his own film in his study. Soumitra would hang a screen on stage and use an actual projector to project the last sequence of his own *Apur Sansar* to create that peerless dramatic effect on stage.

This mixing of two media with such success was hitherto unseen in Bengali theatre, be it the commercial stage or Group Theatre. The strength of Soumitra's belief as a director lay in the fact that he could bind the common audience of commercial theatre with his perception of modern theatre and the depth in his script. It will be unfair and illogical to attribute the relentless box-office success of his plays to his star appeal alone.

In several discussions, Soumitra repeatedly mentioned to me that he believed the public theatre space was where most of the audience would throng. Soumitra was quick to realize that the days of Sisir Bhaduri or Girish Ghosh were no more. The audience changed, and so did their tastes. In cinema, the more popular mass media and the influence of Hindi films were casting long shadows.

Bengali cinema was slowly but surely succumbing to the Hindi onslaught. The popular space in Bengali theatre was shrinking and the cheap commercial aspects in the form of cabaret and fake thrills started becoming regular in the mainstream, commercial theatre of North Calcutta. Unlike the earlier times, none of the popular writers of the '60s and '70s took to writing plays, which created a dearth of quality, contemporary literature on which commercial theatre could have thrived.

As a result, not only Group Theatre, but Soumitra himself, needed to cross shores and look at western plays as a source for his theatre. In his choice of plays, he emphasized that he looked for content with strong narrative bases having twists and undercurrents. In his initial staged plays, from *Naam Jiban* to *Darpane Sarat Sashi* at least, one undercurrent of the narrative remained a conflict arising out of unfulfilled love between the central characters.

Soumitra understood somewhere deep down that, instead of superlative ideologies which might become inaccessible to most of his audience in public theatre, the crux of the narratives in his theatrical productions should revolve around a basic love interest to which the common theatregoer would be able to relate easily. To his credit, Soumitra would transcreate these foreign originals, root them to the Bengali soil and nourish them with vernacular proverbs and adages. In the process, he elevated them to a documentation of the times, included his own ideological and political beliefs, yet kept the basic narrative congruence undisturbed.

***

Unfortunately for Soumitra, most of his so-called friends in Group Theatre couldn't take the popularity of his theatre with the grace it deserved. The quality of the productions and the emotional and ideological gravitas of the plays ensured that they left little room for criticism. A section of the Group Theatre fraternity accused Soumitra of polluting the apparent sanctity of the theatrical stage by exploiting his star image. Farcical as it may sound, most of them jumped into acting in films whenever they got a chance.

What they failed to realize was that Soumitra ventured into theatre not with an amateur mindset out for an evening walk. Theatre was his area of commitment no less than cinema. Rather, in terms of his involvement in its various departments, he was more versatile and engaged in theatre. Most importantly, theatre was providing him with the licence to clarify the self-doubt that cinema was constantly breeding within him. Many of the detractors of the '70s and '80s later turned into his admirers, writing long eulogies adorned with superlatives!

Soumitra in *Andhayug*
(Photo Credit: Bodhisattwa Ghosh)

In spite of the negative vibes, two of the biggest names in Bengali theatre, Ajitesh Banerjee and Utpal Dutt, were a constant support for Soumitra right from the beginning. Earlier, Ajitesh joined Abhinetri Sangha in solidarity with their activities and it was from the Sangha that in February 1971, he directed *Andhayug*, based on a part of the Indian epic Mahabharata, in which Soumitra acted in the role of Ashwatthama. Being a visionary himself, Ajitesh was a support behind Soumitra's bold attempts and modernist approach, which was equally endorsed by Utpal Dutt.

In a lengthy review of *Naam Jiban* in the December '78–January '79 issue of the magazine he edited, *Epic Theatre*, Dutt in his inimitable style wrote: 'In the commercial stage of Kashi Biswanath Mancha, where we have witnessed a number of terrible, covetous and short-sighted endeavours for quite some time, Soumitra Chatterjee sets an unparalleled example of total theatre. A huge set of a slum covering the stage and jutting out of it as well—one can sit on the railings of the stair there and get into a discussion, there is a tap and we can see water fall from it for real, the courtyard where people hang wet clothes regularly, a cycle which is not just a showpiece but is used the way we know it to be.

'There are numerous small items and all of them are used— toothpaste, transistor, a cricket bat, a sewing machine, the news and readings from the radio as a background. The importance and significance of realistic theatre which Stanislavski had presented to the world, and which is sadly missing from our Bengali stage almost always due to our own laziness and crudity, Soumitra has made a stunning attempt to reinstate it…Not only vis-à-vis the barren, bankrupt professional stage, this production, like a forgotten ideal, as if a conscience, holds a light for the entire Bengali theatre and its recent activities, almost like Gorky.'*

Soumitra continued using the stage to its fullest. For *Neelkantho*, staged ten years after *Naam Jiban*, he used a revolving stage for the last climactic scene. Bengali theatre hadn't witnessed many such intelligent usages, one definitely used by Dutt himself in his own *Tiner Talowar*.

Neelkantho found Soumitra at the peak of his thespian acumen on stage. In cinema, he had already established himself by then. In theatre, he had proven his mettle as a playwright and also as a director. To establish himself as one of the finest on the Bengali stage, it took ten years for him and a role like Neelkantho, who is a sluggard. Soumitra, as Neelkantho, toggled between two timeframes—one as a young man favoured by the zamindar's wife and the other, the old, aged self.

One particular scene just before the interval—when a group of young loafers supported by a nouveau-riche, local merchant instigates the aged Neelkantho to drink more in order to unearth the gossips about the aristocratic zamindari—remains etched in every viewer's memory. Soumitra used to deliver a performance where the audience would find him larger than the stage itself as the inner turmoil, the decades-long deprivation and embarrassment spread within his veins and burst out. With sheer silence, the audience would experience a performance as

---

* Arunendra Mukherjee, *Naam Soumitra*, Arkadeep, 1995, pp. 158-159—translated by the author.

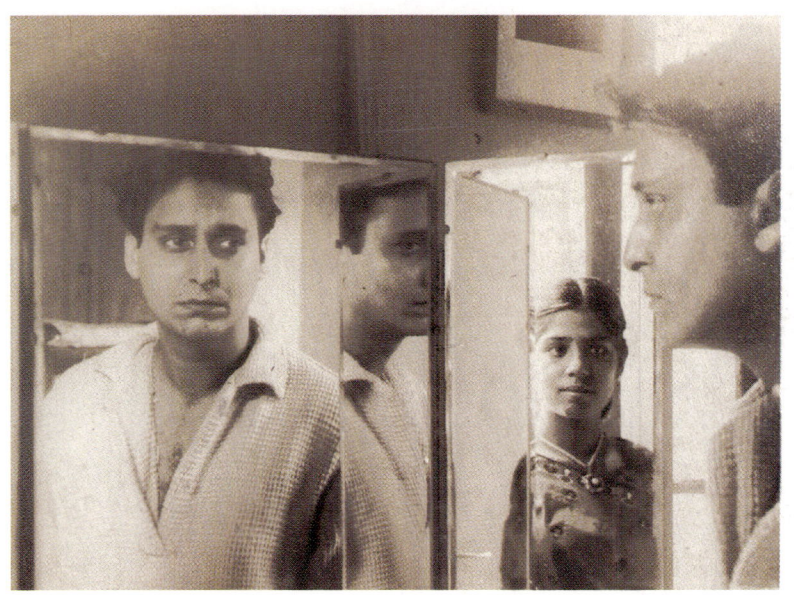
Soumitra and wife Deepa, when young (Credit- Poulami Chatterjee).

Enjoying a light moment with his wife and daughter in the '70s (Credit - Sukumar Roy).

With his son and wife for a dance programme of daughter Poulami (Credit - Sukumar Roy).

Soumitra with his family during a shooting break of Satyajit Ray's 'Ashani Sanket' (Credit- Poulami Chatterjee).

Soumitra directing his daughter Poulami in his telefilm 'Stree ka Patra' (Credit- Poulami Chatterjee).

Soumitra with daughter Poulami in 'Neelkantha' (Credit- Poulami Chatterjee).

Soumitra with his daughter Poulami on the day of her marriage (Credit- Poulami Chatterjee).

With his grandchildren when they were young (Credit - Catherine Berge).

Soumitra with Ismail Merchant during the shooting of 'Gaach' (Credit - Catherine Berge).

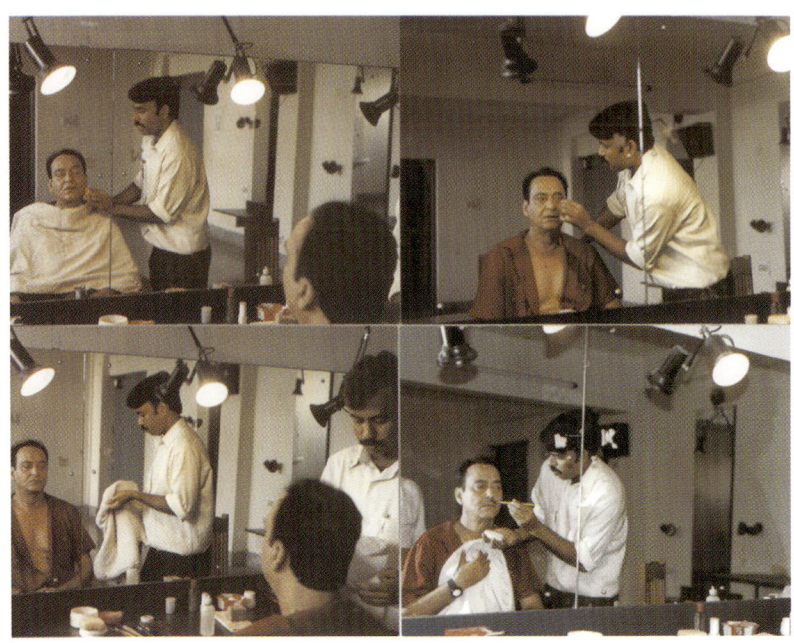

Preparing for a role before a theatre performance
(Credit - Catherine Berge).

Soumitra as Lear (Credit - Minerva Repertory Theatre and Suman Mukherjee).

Soumitra as the film hero Rajkumar in 'Rajkumar'
(Credit- Poulami Chatterjee).

Soumitra with Sharmila Tagore during the shooting of Catherine Berge's 'Gaach' (Credit - Catherine Berge).

Biswajit, Soumitra, Waheeda Rehman and Sumita Sanyal at an award function (Credit - Sukumar Roy).

With Suchitra Sen (Credit - Sukumar Roy).

With his friend Rabi Ghosh during the shooting of 'Gaach' (Credit - Catherine Berge).

With luminaries of Indian Classical music - Ustad Ali Akbar Khan, Ustad Aashish Khan, Ustad Zakir Hussain (Credit- Poulami Chatterjee).

Soumitra Chatterjee at Tagore's House (Credit - Amitava Nag).

Soumitra Chatterjee in 'Peace Haven' (Credit - Suman Ghosh, Amal Kundu).

Vice President Mr Mohd. Hamid Ansari and other dignitaries presenting the Dadasaheb Phalke Award to Soumitra Chatterjee at the 59th National Film Awards on 3 May 2012 (Credit - Press Information Bureau).

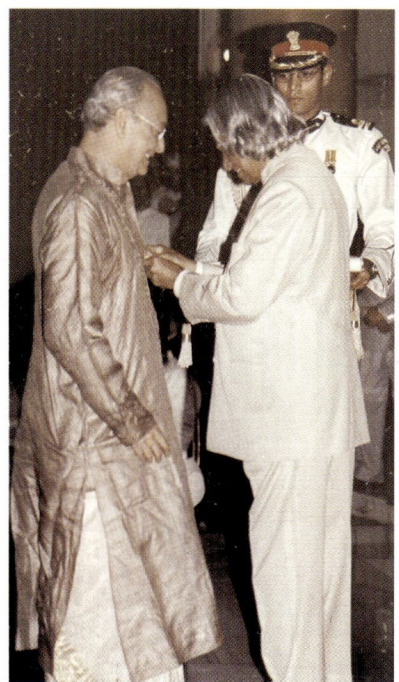

Soumitra being presented with Padma Bhushan by the then President of India Mr A P J Abdul Kalam
(Credit- Poulami Chatterjee).

Soumitra delivering his acceptance speech after being conferred with The Legion of Honour (Credit - Consulate General of France in Kolkata).

The President, Smt. Pratibha Patil presenting the Best Actor Award to Soumitra Chatterjee at the 54th National Film Awards function on 2 September 2008 (Credit - Press Information Bureau).

A cartoon of Soumitra Chatterjee by Kutty
(from the book 'Bishoy Soumitra' published by Ashirbad Prakashani).

A cover of Ekshan (Credit - Amitava Nag).

A painting of Soumitra Chatterjee
(Credit - Jyotirmoy Bhattacharya).

A painting of Soumitra Chatterjee along with 4 lines from his poem
(Credit - Jyotirmoy Bhattacharya).

divine, yet subtle, as a huge cloud hovering over our existence, drenching us. The effect lingered, the performance stayed with the audience even after the actor left the stage.

Those who had the fortune of witnessing Sisir Kumar Bhaduri on stage would swear that it was indeed a height that the legend would have been proud to touch as well. The pupil, playing Neelkantho Lahiri, matched the mentor.

Such a magnificent performance is never easy to achieve, nor is it always possible with the structure of a particular play. Soumitra provoked the same audience response later again when he played the supremo in *Raja Lear*. *Neelkantho* remained one of the three finest performances of Soumitra on stage as an actor. *Raja Lear* was indeed a hallmark of his career, and also of Bengali theatre of all time.

The third best is undoubtedly as the thriller writer Satyasindhu Choudhury in *Tiktiki*. Though unduly miserly with his compliments for Soumitra's acting in his films, Satyajit Ray was ebullient in his praise. 'I like *Neelkantho* the most, from amongst all the plays staged by Soumitra Chatterjee; Soumitra's performance in it is unforgettable.'* To Soumitra, it remained the biggest commendation that he cherished for his histrionics in Bengali theatre.

---

* Amitava Nag, *Beyond Apu: 20 Favourite Film Roles of Soumitra Chatterjee*, HarperCollins Publishers India, 2016, p. 129.

SIX

Beyond Ray

Quite interestingly, even in his long stint in theatre, both on the professional stage and later in Group Theatre, Soumitra never had his own theatre group, though he was close to the groups Ayanda, Prachya and later Shyambajar Mukhomukhi. Way back in 1962, Soumitra formed a theatre group named Ekshan (from the magazine he started editing a year back) which didn't last long and fizzled out without a production of its own. Since the early '70s, when Soumitra started thinking seriously about theatre and his active participation in it with the Abhinetri Sangha productions, he was also involved with another theatre group, Pratikriti.

Incidentally, Pratikriti was a group with which Deepa Chatterjee, Soumitra's wife, was actively involved. Soumitra named the group, guided its members in acting and directed them, although he never acted in any of their productions. The association with Pratikriti started when Soumitra directed

Bidhi o Byatikram for a production in June 1971. Some of their notable creations with Soumitra as the director included *Sree Hari Sahay, Chhoto Bakulpurer Jatri* and *Himalaye Jibanta Manush* between 1972 and 1974.

Incidentally, *Bidhi o Byatikram* was the first time he directed a play that he had translated himself. On the insistence of Sisir Kumar Bhaduri, Soumitra had penned *Bidhi o Byatikram* from Bertolt Brecht's *Exception and the Rule* years earlier.

In the early '60s, when Soumitra was rising to stardom and reshaping his sensitivities, Deepa was making her mark as well. Deepa, like Soumitra, had a rich cultural environment at her paternal home. As a child and then through her teenage years, she was trained in Kathak dance, took singing lessons and learnt to play the sitar. No wonder then that their children took to cultural vocations from a young age—Sougata is a violin player and poet, Poulami a dancer and theatre actor-cum-director.

The real talent of Deepa Chatterjee, however, lay elsewhere. She was keen on badminton since childhood and represented her college, Scottish Church College, Calcutta, in tournaments. After marriage and the birth of Sougata, pursuing badminton was difficult. Perchance, one day, Dipu Ghosh, the reigning Bengal champion and an astounding player at national level throughout the '60s, visited the Chatterjees. He was brought in by another sporting legend, P.K. Banerjee, who happened to be Soumitra's long-time friend. PK, as he was popularly known in his playing days and later in his equally illustrious coaching years, remained Soumitra's friend till his death in 2020, eight months prior to Soumitra's own. Not only PK, and later Dipu, but several other sporting personalities of Bengal were also friends with Soumitra due to his latent knack for sports and natural athleticism.

It was in that meeting that Deepa's badminton laurels were discussed. Dipu, a state-level champion, insisted that they play a match then and there. Soumitra teamed up with PK and Dipu with Deepa. Impressed with her techniques, Dipu asserted that Deepa should consider playing professionally. It was through Dipu's persistence that Deepa's name was enrolled with the badminton association in Bengal in singles as well as mixed doubles, where she teamed up with Dipu.

From 1962 to 1964, Deepa was the champion at the Bengal State Championship. It was her second pregnancy that forced her to withdraw from badminton in the latter part of 1964, as a reigning champion in top form. When Deepa was in full swing, Soumitra would practise with her and other top badminton players of Bengal at the badminton court of South Eastern Railway Club or at the sports facility at the Ordnance Club. Soumitra cherished these sessions and believed that sports in the form of exercise made his body strong yet flexible.

Playing hockey at a second-division club during his college days in the '50s and practising badminton during the early '60s helped Soumitra physically and also in understanding his own physique. He also played badminton against Manoj Guha and Gajanan Hemadi, who were at that time fourth in world ranking for men's doubles. After Deepa retired from competitive sports, Soumitra's stint with badminton slowly waned. Yet, his love for different types of sport remained. A devoted practitioner of yoga, he was a regular spectator at football and cricket matches till the time he could manage visiting them.

Deepa's contribution to Soumitra's life was far reaching. Yet, she always maintained a staid aloofness from his stardom. An artist at heart, Deepa got engaged in stage designs in limited capacities. She also fashioned Soumitra's dresses quite ahead of the times and changed his clothing style altogether.

It was for her group Pratikriti that Deepa was looking for English plays to translate and adapt. It was then that she came across a 1957 play, *Moon on a Rainbow Shawl* by Errol John. Described as 'ground-breaking' soon after its publication, it looked at slum life reeling under poverty and its predominantly black inmates hoping to take flight beyond physical realms. This eternal hope for a better life was what drew Deepa to the play, and she adapted it in Bengali and named her play, *Ramdhanu Ronger Chador*. This was the only play Deepa ever wrote.

When Soumitra decided to plunge full-fledged into professional stage, he borrowed this Bengali transcreation from Deepa, rewrote a few parts and changed the name to *Naam Jiban*. When it was finally staged in the Kashi Biswanath Mancha on 21 December 1978, Deepa's name was not mentioned as the writer due to her vociferous assertion. She strongly believed that sharing her name as the co-writer would give the impression that Soumitra was promoting his wife!

***

For the name of his first regular attempt on the professional stage after establishing himself in cinema, Soumitra depended on his friend Shakti Chatterjee. It was Shakti's poem 'Naam Jiban' which inspired Soumitra to change the name Deepa had initially kept for it. The logo was designed by none other than Satyajit Ray.

Ray had been a source of sustenance, an inspiration to push boundaries and a friend for Soumitra. Asked many times how he would want to describe the relationship, he would find it difficult to articulate it clearly. At times, in the initial days, Ray was a mentor, almost like a father, guiding Soumitra to his maturity as an actor. Later, he was more of a benevolent chaperon who relied on Soumitra to be the face of his views. There was mutual respect and a deep connection.

Ray never had any secretary and managed all his appointments and work on his own. Influenced by him, Soumitra as well never had any secretary to manage his dates even when he was a top draw at the box office. In the cultural space, they moved in step with each other. Ray made films, wrote stories, illustrated magazines and books, edited a children's magazine, *Sandesh*, and provided music to his films. Soumitra acted in films, wrote, directed and acted in plays, recited, edited *Ekshan* and wrote poetry.

Incidentally, the cover design of his first four books of poems published between 1975 and 1983 were all done by Ray. For his fifth, *Haay Chirojol*, published in 1992, when Ray was incapacitated due to his illness, the design was done by another polymath—Purnendu Patrea.

With Ray passing away on 23 April 1992, the world came shattering down for Soumitra. He admitted the same day on television that he had become fatherless for the second time in his life. Not only as an actor in cinema, Soumitra's indebtedness to Ray was paramount. It was more like family. Ray had presented his grandfather's violin to Sougata when Sougata started performing in functions. When Soumitra requested for pointers to get initiated in Western classical music, Ray provided him with a list with the order in which he should listen to the music that benefitted the actor. Soumitra gained from this counselling and that reflected in his selection of music for his plays later.

Even before embarking on *Apur Sansar*, Ray had asked Soumitra what he would do with his job in All India Radio. Soumitra was categorical that he would leave the job to act in the film. Ray thoughtfully remarked then that he could cast Soumitra for his future films as well but that would not be enough for the young man to pay his bills. Eventually, Soumitra spread his wings wider than Ray's films alone. Yet, through each decade of their association, Ray consistently cast him from a young man to a mature doctor in *Ganashatru* and the mentally challenged second brother in his penultimate film, *Shakha Prashakha*.

Most of the other prominent directors including Tapan Sinha and Mrinal Sen found their protagonist in Soumitra in the '60s. Both cast Soumitra again, much later, in the mid-'80s and after. Probably, only Satyajit Ray had this inexplicable bond with Soumitra which transcended a mere professional attachment. This director-actor duo is unique and peerless in the history of world cinema precisely for their length of relationship and its quality.

Soumitra's association with Ray is most famously equated with the working relationship between the Japanese duo of Toshiro Mifune and Akira Kurosawa, and the Swedish one of

Max von Sydow and Ingmar Bergman. But in these comparisons, what most of the critics miss out is the proper context. Mifune had been a stupendous support to Kurosawa without a doubt. But in terms of numbers and considering the gamut of roles of older people that he got, much more than Mifune, it was Takashi Shimura who has a closer semblance with Soumitra.

Unlike Mifune, who relied on physical acting, Shimura and Soumitra banked on a more subdued rendition. Mifune and Kurosawa ran into differences and the former slowly faded away from Kurosawa's later films the same way Max von Sydow remained with Bergman only as a young hero. For the older characters, the Swede maestro depended more frequently on Erland Josephson.

On the other hand, Ray continued with Soumitra as the young dreamer in *Apur Sansar* to the disillusioned and elderly doctor in *Ganashatru*. It will not be unjust to hence conclude that Ray depended on Soumitra the same way Soumitra relied on him for meaningful roles throughout the three decades of their creative partnership.

When Soumitra was acting as an arrogant Rajput taxi driver in *Abhijan*, Ray told him his plans of making *Ashani Sanket* and casting him as the docile Bengali priest, Gangacharan. Ray finally did so after almost twelve years. Similarly, Sandip in *Ghare Baire*, a negative character, was discussed for more than two decades before finally materializing as one of Soumitra's most sophisticated renditions. Soon after Ray's literary creation, Feluda, started becoming popular, Ray deliberately made the illustrations resemble Soumitra. Later, in 1974, when he made *Sonar Kella*, the first of his two Feluda films, it was neither a surprise for Soumitra nor the readers of the detective stories who readily identified him with the sleuth.

Yet, Ray, on several other occasions, refused Soumitra roles which he wanted in his films. When Ray was hunting for actors to play Goopy in the eloquent *Goopy Gyne Bagha Byne*, Soumitra had already acted in six of his films in ten years. But the profile of Goopy was that of a poor village farmer which needed to have a certain raw, rural look which Soumitra lacked given his fine features. Ray was unwilling and Soumitra kept on assuring Ray that he would do a good job if given a chance. Ray agreed that Soumitra would act well as Goopy but didn't relent, finally stating that the mental image of the character in his mind didn't match with Soumitra's profile.

Soumitra was crestfallen. Not only was Goopy an extremely endearing character but, more importantly, it would have added a new dimension to the varied profiles he had acted in so far. On its release, after watching Tapen Chatterjee playing the role with extraordinary finesse—with his rustic looks complementing the character—Soumitra conceded that it would have been immensely difficult for him to match Tapen's performance.

However, *Goopy Gyne Bagha Byne* wasn't the first film which Soumitra wanted from Ray and couldn't act in. *Kanchenjungha* was Ray's first colour film which addresses the moral decadence of the affluent Bengali middle class of a time when they prided in their mimicry of the West. For the role of a young jobless Ashok, Ray initially thought of Soumitra. Unfortunately, Soumitra had already committed dates of shooting for another film which clashed with the ones of *Kanchenjungha*. Ray then chose Arun Mukherjee to portray the character.

Later, when Soumitra went to meet Ray after the latter had returned from shooting in the mountains, Ray jokingly told Soumitra that it was good for the film that Soumitra didn't act in it. Realizing that Soumitra was probably upset by the remark, Ray explained that being a romantic hero already, Soumitra's casting as Ashok would have robbed the open-ended possibilities of the film. Despite its ending, Ray feared that the audience would have assumed an emerging love-story once the central characters meet in Calcutta later.

Soumitra was also extremely keen to play Manmohan in Ray's last film, *Agantuk*. Ray declined and the role went to Utpal Dutt. Like Goopy, this time as well, Ray didn't agree with Soumitra playing a profile that did not match his own mental image of the character. Spot-on again, Ray explained that given Soumitra's popular, benevolent image, the audience would be tempted to believe that the stranger could not be anything but a nice, honest person. Ray elaborated that a person with the kind of image Utpal Dutt had in films would be able to sustain the suspense surrounding the character.

For his next film, *Uttaran*, Ray however thought of Soumitra again as an honest doctor, faced with a dilemma about his profession and meaning in the context of society at large. He completed the script, finalized the casting but passed away before the film's shooting started. Later, it was executed by his son Sandip. Soumitra mentioned to me time and again that not a day passed when he didn't remember his beloved 'Manik-da' for one reason or other. Ray was omnipresent in Soumitra's mind, till the end.

***

On the night of Saturday, 12 October 1991, at the prestigious Star Theatre in North Calcutta, Soumitra Chatterjee and Madhabi Mukherjee acted in *Ghatak Biday*, written and directed by Soumitra himself as usual. It was the night of Maha Choturthi, the fourth auspicious day leading to Bengal's very own Durga Puja festival. The performance ended shortly after nine in the evening like every other night. Starting on 9 September the previous year and being the first comedy after four serious plays, *Ghatak Biday* was Soumitra's most successful production till then as far as box office returns were concerned. When the last stage show was performed on 5 July 1992, there were nearly 600 productions already and almost all had been houseful.

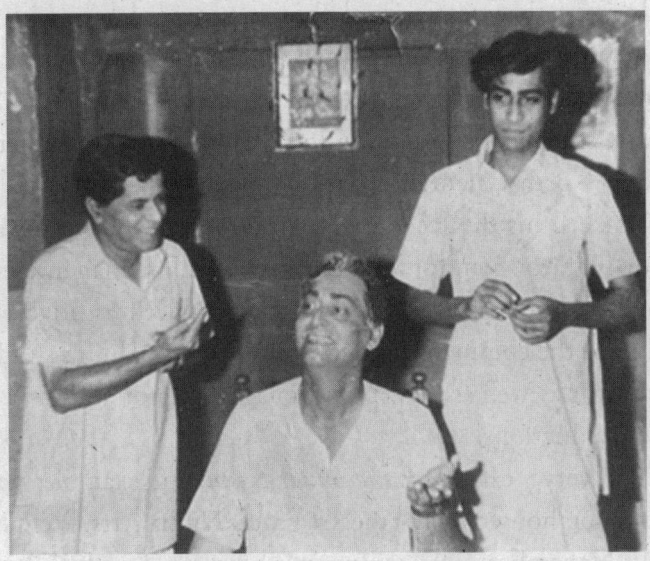

Soumitra with veteran actor Rabi Ghosh and Kaushik Sen in *Ghatak Biday*
(Photo Credit: Poulami Chatterjee)

On that fateful night, after the stroke of twelve, around 1:30 a.m. on Sunday, 13 October 1991, a devastating fire broke out in Star Theatre and gutted the entire building. No one was injured and the only casualty was a piece of heritage in Bengali professional theatre founded near the very end of the nineteenth century and which saw all prominent Bengali theatre actors on its stage, starting with Girish Ghosh.

For Soumitra, it was a huge personal loss. Not only did he debut as a professional theatre actor in Star with *Tapasi* in 1963, but most importantly, this fire sounded the death knell for his association with the professional stage.

Soumitra had always believed in staging his theatre within the ambit of the commercial, professional board of Bengali theatre instead of the more elite Group Theatre at that time. He insisted that professional theatre provided him with the opportunity of entertaining the maximum with his brand of intelligent and thoughtful entertainment. The fire at Star Theatre somehow ended Soumitra's tryst with the commercial stage of North Calcutta.

To keep his theatre going, Soumitra soon looked towards Group Theatre. Some of these groups were more than interested to have Soumitra stage plays in their productions. Like what he did for the commercial stage, Soumitra brought his stardom as an actor as well as his reputation as a director and writer to these productions.

The very next, *Darpane Sarat Sashi*, for example, was a production housed by the theatre group Nibha Arts. Premiered on 26 November 1992 at Tapan Theatre in South Calcutta, it was the first play which Soumitra directed and acted in but did not write. Penned by Manoj Mitra, *Darpane Sarat Sashi* looked at the glorious past of Bengali theatre of the last century. Ironical that to pay a tribute to North Calcutta's commercial Bengali theatre, which he revered, Soumitra needed to stage this play from a Group Theatre platform in South Calcutta!

Soumitra reached his pinnacle as a writer-director-actor in theatre with *Tiktiki* in 1995. Based on Anthony Shaffer's 1970 play, *Sleuth*, *Tiktiki* is a psychological thriller involving only two characters—an aged crime fiction writer and a young upcoming man apparently in a love relationship with the writer's young wife. *Sleuth* was made into a critically successful film with the same name starring Sir Lawrence Olivier and Michael Caine. But there is a history to *Tiktiki*.

In the '70s, when Soumitra was deeply involved with Abhinetri Sangha and staging plays to raise money, Utpal Dutt directed *Crushbiddho Cuba* for the Sangha which involved over forty actors and actresses. Since all its performers were film actors and actresses, it soon became difficult to organize shows due to conflicts in available dates. Soumitra, being the secretary of Abhinetri Sangha, requested Dutt to choose a different play that they could stage more frequently. After much deliberation, Dutt suggested *Sleuth* on the condition that the adaptation had to be done by Soumitra himself. Soumitra agreed.

It was decided that Dutt would direct the play with Soumitra playing the younger character and Dutt the older one. However, after being suitably adapted, the play couldn't be performed by Abhinetri Sangha. There were a few other options about a group producing it, including Dutt's own People's Little Theatre, but none materialized in the end.

Interestingly, Soumitra sounded Uttam Kumar out as well. The latter was reportedly attracted to it. Uttam maintained that he wouldn't be able to do a theatre performance considering his health and the fact that both the characters were on stage throughout the almost three-hour play. He suggested that Soumitra direct a film from the script. Uttam even advised Soumitra to sound out a few film producers in whose production companies they both had a few blockbuster hits.

Unfortunately, none of the producers seemed interested in a plot devoid of song sequences and, more importantly, without a heroine. It is rather sad that no Bengali producer could look ahead and appreciate the novelty of this project—a film with two of the best actors of the country and directed by one of them. Much later, after almost two decades, when a new theatre group, Swapnasandhani, was struggling to make its mark, Soumitra gave them a huge boost by agreeing to perform *Tiktiki* on stage for the first time. Obviously, by then he had moved to the role of the older character while Kaushik Sen, founder of Swapnasandhani, played the younger one.

Tiktiki remains one of Soumitra's very best. A script of the highest order, Soumitra mixed it with ethnic elements, the psychological slants between 'Bangals' (migrants from East Bengal) and 'Ghatis' (natives of West Bengal), interspersed with proverbs and idioms. To top it all, the production had an extravagant set designed by Soumitra with an acting standard that very few theatre productions of the time could match. It will not be an exaggeration to say that Soumitra's characterization had more range, more depth of emotion and more subtlety than the one played by the legendary Sir Olivier.

***

With the demise of Satyajit Ray, Soumitra's hopes of getting worthy roles reduced further. His appearances in the films of his other favourite directors had waned over time already. Yet, thanks to his character roles since the mid-'80s, he was being considered for elderly roles. Tapan Sinha's *Atanka* played a major part in Soumitra's acceptance for roles more advanced than his physical age. Raja Mitra's *Ekti Jiban* in 1990 is one such, for instance, with epic proportions.

The central character in *Ekti Jiban* is that of a Bengali lexicographer who takes on the mammoth mission of compiling the first authentic dictionary in the language. Set in the 1930s, the film captures the man's journey and relentless struggle against all odds, both personal and professional, from the

Raja Mitra directing Soumitra with Kamal Nayek
behind the lens in *Ekti Jiban*
(Photo Credit: Shyamal Karmakar)

pre-Partition uncertainties to the hardships of a refugee life. Spanning a few decades from his middle-age to a very advanced one when he finally receives recognition, Soumitra is Gurudas Bhattacharya every inch.

Incidentally, Satyajit Ray once wished to make a film out of the novel by Buddhadeb Basu. Ray, however, was sceptical about the quality of make-up available in Bengali cinema at that time that was required to convey an actor ageing over decades. He initially thought of taking Kanu Banerjee (Harihar of *Pather Panchali*) who would have fitted in nicely in the older age. But to make him look young was a difficult task with make-up.

The opposite was a problem he envisioned if he took on Soumitra for the role. Eventually, Ray had to shelve the idea. Raja Mitra took it up much later. In an interview to me earlier, Mitra reminisced, 'I wanted an educated and sensitive actor, and could think of no one but Soumitra Chatterjee at the time. When I met Soumitra-da to offer him the role, he surprised me by going to his study and bringing out the two volumes of the dictionary written by Haricharan Bandyopadhyay, on whom the character of Gurudas is based. Browsing through the pages, I found that there were several notes in the margins, and I knew at that moment that no one could be more fitting for the role.'*

Since there were several scenes showing him writing the dictionary, Soumitra, much like what he did for Amal in *Charulata*, practised writing with the old type of pens before

---

* Amitava Nag, *Beyond Apu: 20 Favourite Film Roles of Soumitra Chatterjee*, HarperCollins Publishers India, 2016, p. 107.

fountain pens became common. The film was shot for over six years due to budgetary constraints, and at times there were gaps of more than six to eight months between shoots.

Soumitra's mastery and control over the vocation was such that there were never any issues with continuity in bringing the character alive. As always, he would read the script multiple times, remembering the nuances and behavioural features that he inculcated in the character.

For the very old phase, Soumitra went through an arduous make-up that used to take six hours to be applied and another three to remove. Raja Mitra, the director, was effusive in his praise for Soumitra, the actor and the human being. Mitra always mentions how cooperative Soumitra had been even when he was not paid on time, and even then, did not get the full amount. On a number of occasions, Soumitra confessed to me how when he would see the worth of a role, he was ready to compromise on his normal fees. Much later, when he had to churn out repetitive performances in trivial, forgettable roles, he would lament his decision to forego financial benefits at times. It is worth speculating if a trip to Bollywood would probably have saved him from several embarrassing encounters on-screen in the Bengali film industry.

After *Atanka*, Soumitra became the go-to man for Tapan Sinha. It was surprising why he never thought of using Soumitra for more than twenty years in between. Probably, like a few others, he also considered Soumitra more in Satyajit Ray's team and was hesitant to cast him oftener than he did. In *Antardhan*, Soumitra consolidated his newly nurtured image of the middle-class, educated, retired teacher. But his zenith of success in a Sinha film came in *Wheel Chair*. As in *Kony*, Soumitra breathed life into the profile of a mentor, a doctor in this case, confined to a wheelchair.

To get behind the skin of a physically incapacitated person, Soumitra practised using the wheelchair for many months. He realized that anyone confined to a wheelchair must have a very different perception of things. The mere fact that they must look up at people during any communication creates a difference in physical levels and has a psychological impact.

The latent student in Soumitra helped him learn new things about life and his craft continuously. After Ray's demise, he would visit Sinha often and, on many occasions, the two spent time watching an old Hollywood classic with Sinha analysing the acting schemes in minute detail. Sinha, like Ray, was a master of handling actors and understood the core of the craft of an actor. In a scene in *Wheel Chair*, one of the inmates donates a huge sum of money. At the time of rehearsals, Soumitra's reaction was that of surprise and, to an extent, disbelief in receiving such generosity. Accordingly, he looked up in a flash with an expression of astonishment.

Sinha walked up to Soumitra and whispered to him that given the level of surprise, almost like a shock, a reaction could be either very fast or very slow. Soumitra realized Sinha's bird's-eye view of the character and the situation, and in the final take, he followed the action very slowly. Soumitra's rendition of the character was so accurate that after watching the film, a paraplegic on a wheelchair thanked him and certified the authenticity of the portrayal.

***

Along with the trinity of Satyajit Ray, Ritwik Ghatak and Mrinal Sen, a host of prominent directors including Tapan Sinha, Ajoy Kar, Asit Sen, Rajen Tarafdar, Tarun Majumder and others sustained the overall quality of Bengali cinema for three decades from the '50s till the late '70s. Since the early '80s, a host of younger filmmakers started directing films. Most notable among them were Buddhadeb Dasgupta, Goutam Ghose, Utpalendu Chakraborty and Aparna Sen.

Their preference for cinema mostly stemmed from narrative modes of storytelling, apart from Dasgupta's to an extent, who explored and experimented beyond the traditional narratives. Thematically, apart from Aparna Sen, others were probably philosophically closer to Mrinal Sen than both Satyajit Ray and Ritwik Ghatak. Accordingly, neither do we find them dealing with the upper middle-class milieu as in Ray nor do they get hooked to the identity of a race devastated by political bungling as in Ghatak.

Soumitra understandably found himself left out of the serious cinema of this younger generation of Bengali filmmakers. In the '80s and then the next decade, he was still relying on a Ray, a Sen or a Tapan Sinha film to offer him challenges. In several interviews in the '90s, he lamented that the younger directors didn't find him suitable for their films.

Most of them agreed that Soumitra was not fitting into their scheme of things. He was yet to attain the status of a Chhabi Biswas, who garnered the conviction of filmmakers in the late '50s to write scripts keeping his age in mind. That list included Satyajit Ray more than once.

It doesn't come as a surprise that the first time Soumitra

was cast in a film of one of the prominent younger filmmakers, it was in a Rituparno Ghosh film—*Asukh* in 1999. Ghosh was even younger than Goutam, Buddhadeb, Utpalendu or Aparna. He blazed into cinema with *Unishe April* in 1994. (His first film, *Hirer Angti*, was rather insipid at the box office and didn't get an official release.) He soon consolidated his place in Indian cinema with multiple National Awards for each of his first few films.

For middle-class Bengalis, Ghosh was important. Ray and Ghatak had passed away, Sinha and Sen were no longer making films. A section of middle-class Bengalis couldn't connect with the cinema of Goutam, Buddhadeb or Utpalendu and soon started moving away from the cinema hall. Rituparno Ghosh filled this vacuum blending the sensibilities of the cinema of Ray and Sinha.

As an aged father of a film heroine, Soumitra is flawless in *Asukh*. He was not the central character, though he was an important one. For the role, Rituparno wanted Soumitra to break his elegant walking style to suit the character. The film's narrative premise had an inherent flaw that prevented it from soaring the heights of many of Rituparno's other films. Yet, Soumitra's portrayal of the aged father was spot-on.

A trend that started with *Atanka*, a decade and a half back, became an established norm since *Asukh*. With the turn of the new millennium, and with newer and younger directors coming up, Soumitra became a constant feature. He had few rivals when he played the Bengali youth in the '60s and '70s. Since 2000, he was peerless as the aged face of the beaten Bengali psyche.

SEVEN

New Millennium, Newer Challenges

Asukh made Soumitra Chatterjee accessible to younger filmmakers. Though he didn't act in many films of serious directors of the '80s, he soon became more regular with the millennial ones. Aparna Sen cast him for the first time in *Paromitar Ekdin* in an important yet short role. The role of a defeated suitor, a second choice for an independent-minded woman due to his own obvious, short-sighted anxiety, was cut out for Soumitra's image. His was the epitome of the defeated other vis-à-vis Uttam Kumar's conquer and command aura in the audience's mind. The character of Moni-da in *Paromitar Ekdin*, with his indecisions, vacillations and uncertainties is as if an extension of Amitava in Satyajit Ray's *Kapurush*.

However, Soumitra's portrayal as the blind poet and intellectual Sashi Bhushan in Goutam Ghose's *Dekha* in 2001 remains one of the finest performances of the thespian.

Any actor of repute has almost always used his or her eyes to great effect in portraying different emotions of the character. Soumitra himself has used them to realize Apu or Amal's dreams, the anger of Narsingh, the sharp brilliance of Feluda or the helplessness of the schoolteacher in *Atanka*.

In *Dekha*, as Sashi Bhushan is blind, Soumitra ensured that in lieu of his expressive eyes, he made the whole face act to convey the subtle and at times contradictory expressions of a very complex character. In addition, there are several monologues and soliloquies in which Soumitra excels, helping us understand Sashi's mental state.

Like he did for Tapan Sinha's *Wheel Chair*, Soumitra took great care to understand the psychology of blind people and observe the nuances and variations in their expressions for his character in *Dekha* as well. At the same time, he consulted some doctors to understand how glaucoma spreads and blinds a person who is not blind from birth. For a model to build his character, Soumitra depended on Mr Sadhan Gupta, who happened to be a close acquaintance.

Mr Gupta was the first blind person to become an MP in India and the first to become an advocate general as well. He was also an eminent barrister and a communist till his death. Soumitra's closeness to Mr Gupta helped him pick up behavioural traits from the latter, even if unconsciously. Being involved in several associations and societies that work with blind people long before he acted in *Dekha* indirectly helped Soumitra give the character the necessary cadence.

Dekha was awarded the National Award for Best Bengali Feature film in 2001, and Soumitra Chatterjee was conferred with a special jury award for a realistic portrayal of the scion of a fading aristocracy who has lost his eyesight. Goutam Ghose rejected the award following allegations of nepotism and foul play. Soumitra followed suit. He was reportedly pained and felt insulted for what he considered an attempt to appease him so late in his career by announcing a special jury award.

Goutam repeated Soumitra two years later in *Abar Aranye*, a tribute film to Satyajit Ray's *Aranyer Din Ratri* of 1970. Goutam has constantly mentioned how Soumitra's opulent and varied experience as a thinking artist enriched him and others in his film unit. While filming *Kalbela*, he remembers one such scene in which his childhood friend Bhabani Prasad Dey played the role of a police officer. Soumitra was done with his work that day and while on his way out, he noticed Bhabani dressed up in the uniform.

Goutam reminisces, 'Soumitra-da told Bhabani, „The uniform you are wearing is wrong. At that time, which is depicted in the film, names of officers were not displayed on their chest. Also, the cap is worn in a wrong way." He then called the dresser and explained the changes. Finally, he advised Bhabani to show me the changes first for approval.'*

***

Soumitra was decorated with the best actor award the highest number of times by BFJA (Bengal Film Journalists' Association),

---

* Goutam Ghose, 'Representative of the Bengal Renaissance', *Bichitrapatra: Soumitra Smaran Sankhya*, Third Year First Issue, December 2020, p. 76—translated by the author.

the oldest film critic association in the country founded in 1937. Unfortunately, his tryst with the national film awards had always been lukewarm. He was conferred the special jury award a few times for *Antardhan*, *Wheel Chair*, *Dekha* but was never given the highest award in acting. He could have received it quite a few times for the several masterful roles that he essayed since 1967 when the award was instituted. He didn't care much for the awards later.

Since early on, Soumitra had an apathy for state felicitations. He refused the Padma Shree award first in 1970. When the government officials visited him to confirm his acceptance, Soumitra politely declined them and requested the central government to intervene in the recurring problems that plagued the Bengali film industry back then. In 1992, he was approached again but Soumitra declined this time as well. He felt that the award had lost its credibility since numerous sycophants had been showered with it.

He, however, accepted the Padma Bhushan, which is a higher honour than the Padma Shree, in 2004. Later, in 2012, he also accepted the Dadasaheb Phalke Award, the highest award in cinema in India. When asked why he accepted these two awards, he categorically mentioned that he felt these were less corrupt. Soumitra added that he also felt compelled not to disappoint his fans by rejecting any national award of significant stature that came his way.

Soumitra's avowed inclination towards communism ensured that he was never in the good books of the ruling powers in New Delhi. Jagannath Basu recalled one incident of Soumitra's 'non-compliance' with power when the state of Emergency was declared in 1975. Basu had recently joined Akash Vani Kolkata a year ago as a playwright-in-charge. He was ordered to collect signatures of ten prominent Bengali actors in a statement mentioning that they agreed with the central government's stance and would give their moral support to the government. After convincing the actors, the statement needed to be faxed to the central Ministry of Information and Broadcasting.

Basu recollected, 'Accordingly, a producer of plays in Doordarshan (a famous theatre actor-director) and I went to the actors' houses to save our jobs. Some of the actors known to be respected leftist sympathizers and philosophers agreed immediately. When a few others were a bit reluctant in the beginning, we had to assure them diplomatically that Akash Vani-Doordarshan would look after them in times of crises and job opportunities would come their way if they paid heed.

'We couldn't convince just one person. Soumitra Chatterjee reprimanded us a little and said,„ I will never sign this! I don't need to receive any favour from the government.„ Recently, after he left, I saw a picture of Soumitra signing on the anti-citizenship law platform on paper. This memory of four and a half decades ago rushed back to me. Nowadays, in many cases, I find intellectuals, actors and celebrities crawling in front of one or the other government. Soumitra was truly exceptional.'*

Soumitra may have lost out on a few national awards. The Padma Bhushan and Dadasaheb Phalke came at the dusk of

---

* Jagannath Basu, 'Letters to the Editor', *Anandabazar Patrika*, 25 November 2020. Accessed at https://www.anandabazar.com/editorial/letters-to-the-editor/letters-to-the-editor-character-of-demised-actor-soumitra-chatterjee-1.1233782—translated by the author.

his career. But his impact on the Bengali psyche was so deep that he was conferred honorary DLitt from almost all the leading universities of West Bengal, including Rabindra Bharati University, Burdwan University, Vidyasagar University, Kalyani University, Deshikottam from Visva Bharati University, Bengal Engineering and Science University and Jadavpur University.

He was an international actor in every sense of the term. Soumitra received a Lifetime Achievement Award in the International Film Festival, Napoli, Italy, in 1999 and the 'Ordre des Arts et des Lettres' awarded by the French government the next year. But to top it all, the French government conferred on him the highest civilian award of the country, 'Légion d'honneur', in 2018, three decades after Satyajit Ray received it.

Soumitra treasured individual acclamation more than the institutional ones. On 9 August 1990, on the occasion of a retrospective of Soumitra Chatterjee's films organized by Cine Central, Calcutta, Satyajit Ray gave a written note that read, 'I don't think there is any need to give a certificate to Soumitra. Of my twenty-seven films, Soumitra featured in the main roles in fourteen. This itself will prove what trust I have in him and how I value him as an actor. I do know that to the last day of my artist's life, my dependence on him will remain intact.'*

This to Soumitra was one of the highest compliments that he received. He was also enamoured by audience's reactions a number of times. In many discussions, he would proudly recollect how a wheelchair-bound person felt he was one

---

* Amitava Nag, *Beyond Apu: 20 Favourite Film Roles of Soumitra Chatterjee*, HarperCollins Publishers India, 2016, p. 138.

of them after watching *Wheel Chair*, or how the wife of a blind person came up to him and tearfully acknowledged the authenticity of his portrayal in *Dekha*, or how a taxi driver refused to take the fare from him after *Abhijan*. Time and again, Soumitra emphasized that this love from his audience was what kept him working for six decades.

He mentioned to me about a letter from the daughter of a prostitute. The young girl was fascinated by *Sansar Simante* and Aghor's character. Though the film ended in tragedy, for a while, the petty thief Aghor was a beacon of hope to the prostitute Rajani. The young girl wrote in her letter, 'Society tries to throttle us, defile us. Yet, I am studying against all odds, in search of dignity. As I grow old, I dream of taking my mother away where she can live with some self-respect. I am sending you my deepest regards, reverence and wishes. I am requesting you to send me a photo of you as Aghor. Not for any ill intention. I have liked the character of Aghor a lot and only because of that, I am asking for this. Please don't neglect me as young, and kindly don't redirect the letter back to my address. Because if my mother reads this letter, she will be very sad finding her mention in it.'

On another occasion, when the organizers and local dignitaries showered Soumitra with accolades and praises after his Bengali poetry recitation for an hour and half, an elderly woman came up to him. She was a terminally ill patient who thanked the almighty for keeping her alive to experience such an event. Soumitra never met that woman again in his life but she made a permanent mark on his mind.

He later told me, 'Institutional recognitions invite a lot of media coverage and testimonials from celebrities. I do enjoy them a lot as well. But after a while, I forget them unlike such moments from the so-called common people of my language. Probably, no award can be bigger than the one that helps people in their own struggles to survive and beat the odds.'

***

Two Ghoshs—Atanu and Suman—rose to prominence as filmmakers in the new millennium. Atanu had already made a mark with a number of short films for television. Soumitra acted in a few of them as well. For his first feature film, *Angshumaner Chhabi* in 2009, Atanu had Soumitra play the main role of a retired film actor. He became a regular in Atanu's films from then on till *Mayurakshi* in 2017.

Suman, on the other hand, is a teacher of economics in the Florida Atlantic University. His debut film, *Podokkhep* in 2006, won the National award for the best feature film in Bengali. More importantly, it is for *Podokkhep* that Soumitra won his only best actor award at the 54th National Film Awards. Like Atanu, Suman kept faith in Soumitra in a number of films throughout the next one and a half decades.

Podokkhep deserves special mention, mostly because it provided the necessary endorsement of Soumitra's brilliance in playing senior citizens on screen. It also raises a question about the entire system of lobbying and bias in deciding the awards, against which Soumitra himself raised a voice time and again. The grapevine has it that a few significantly important veteran film personalities felt that it was never too late to consider Soumitra for the award. A jury member, we are told, telephoned Soumitra and asked if he would accept the award. Only then the announcement would be made. Soumitra's reaction to the special jury awards in previous cases had made them sceptical—understandably.

Podokkhep was inspired by a short story, 'The Curious Case of Benjamin Button', written by F. Scott Fitzgerald. The narrative deals with the cycle of life of an individual as he becomes childlike at the very end. The film dwells on this idea and expands it by showing the conflicts between generations and the resulting loneliness of a widowed septuagenarian. As old age smothers Sasanka (played by Soumitra), he loses one of his close friends. At home, bored and frustrated with the world

Suman Ghosh directs Soumitra Chatterjee and co-actor in *Podokkhep* for which he received the Best Actor Award at the National Film Awards.
(Photo Credit: Suman Ghosh)

around him, he is stifled. It is with the help of a five-year-old girl whose family moves in as his neighbours that Sasanka finds meaning in his life. He now wishes to brush aside the agonies and keep pace with the changing times.

With the turn of the century, more and more young Bengali executives started taking jobs away from home, and settling down in other states of the country and also foreign shores. Older parents were left behind to wait for their children's occasional visits home. Wherever they stayed back with the parents, there was a clash of beliefs, a conflict of ideologies between the traditional and the modern. Though such migrations did happen throughout the last century as well, it was not prominent in the Bengali culture the way it became in the new millennium.

In the films of Satyajit Ray, Mrinal Sen, Ritwik Ghatak or Tapan Sinha, the discord was introspective but the points of view had generally been that of the younger generation. At best, they were evenly balanced out between the two. What essentially changed in the psyche of this filmic trend post-2000 was the fact that now the parents became the central characters. It was their loneliness, old age, struggles and survival which formed the narrative core of these films.

The younger ones came and went, like cameos, to lend background to the toils and labour of the older ones. In this shift of focus, Soumitra became the de facto representation of a class and generation. Where *Podokkhep* scores is in lending that extra edge where such an elderly person cycles back to life.

***

Soumitra was always a fast learner. He himself admitted several times that his advantage over a few other contemporaries was how he could learn from the better directors and incorporate their teachings, though at times indirect, in his acting method. This is why, unlike many of his contemporaries, he suited all forms of media—television, theatre and the Bengali folk 'jatra'. Even before the shooting of *Apur Sansar* started, Soumitra was well versed with Stanislavski's acting techniques. In addition, Satyajit Ray had lent his copy of V.I. Pudovkin's *Film Technique and Film Acting* for Soumitra to read.

Early on, Soumitra understood the role of camera and that of light in cinema. It is light rays with varying frequencies that create the magical projections on film strips. He realized that the objective of light is not merely to make an actor visible on screen. In the era of black-and-white, when Soumitra started his journey, the light and shade created different hues within the monochrome. Watching classics and observing Ray at work, Soumitra picked up the finer nuances of exploiting light as an organic component of his work.

Though the lighting scheme is more of a director-cameraman's lookout, better actors have always been aware how their expressions can enhance the creativity of a scene in conjunction with the light arrangement. Appreciating the importance of lighting helped him understand the related techniques on stage later when he started directing professionally.

Not only lighting, for Soumitra it was crucial to understand that, in cinema, camera is the medium that delivers and translates an actor's work to the audience. He readily picked up the nuances of lenses, the different possibilities of different angles, the zooms—all that is necessary and has to be aligned with the actor's own shaping of a role. Equally important is the role of editing in cinema, and how the actor's work is ultimately at the mercy of the finesse of a good editor.

In one of our discussions, he explained, 'Acting is a mode of communication. The camera establishes the actor in different perspectives—sometime indoor, at other times outdoor. As an actor, my preparedness demands that I need to know the position of the camera and what part of my body and which side of it is within the frame. I need to adapt my acting style in accordance with that. If it is a close-up, my expressions will be limited. Otherwise, it will be demonic on-screen. Again, in a long shot, I have to express more.

'In theatre, this distance is mostly constant. So, the degree of expression is different in different media. As an actor, I am more theatrical when I act in theatre and that is what it has to be. Yet, people say I "underact" or act "naturally" in theatre. As you can understand, that can never happen. What I do, with so many years of experience, is that I can create an illusion of "naturalism" on stage even when I am actually expressing it theatrically.'

Being a stage actor prior to embarking as a film one, Soumitra had precise clarity about the principal requirement for acting both on stage and on screen. He explained time and again that the struggle of an actor is to preserve and portray the unity of image of his character. In theatre, if the challenge is to preserve a uniform communication of expression among the audience sitting at different distances from the stage, and to 'theatricalize' the relatively sublime moments of expression, in cinema, the onus is to maintain a continuity of expression when the shooting process is discontinuous and non-sequential. When Soumitra acted in 'jatra' or the one-wall productions with three sides open (instead of a theatre production within a confined auditorium), he had to amplify his expressions many times more than what he could afford to in theatre.

To explain the degree of difference in acting across the different media, Soumitra's favourite analogy was always painting. He would cite how impressionist paintings express the reality of our daily lives without following realistic lines. Then, in cubism, the style is totally changed yet the objective is to express the real conditions of human existence. In the same vein, acting also requires different styles as one embraces different media.

Irrespective of the advantages or challenges of different media, the basic truth which remains unchanged is the fact that acting is a representation of reality. It thrives from imitation of life by creating an illusion of someone else's reality or a semblance of it. At the core of it, the reality of any art blooms on some aspect of reality of the human existence. Soumitra had always searched for such an internal truth in most of the significant characters he portrayed. It was through this search for truth that he could get to the very heart of the roles, internalize them and express them on screen or in front of his audience with effortless ease.

After he acted in Sujoy Ghosh's *Ahalya*, a fourteen-minute thriller which was released on YouTube in 2015, Soumitra told me how he loved acting in challenging roles even at the ripe age of eighty. To him, the format—be it digital or celluloid—the length being feature or short was less important. 'To me, what is important is each individual shot. The techniques of acting based on technology are minor adjustments. Between stage and cinema, you need to shift more gears. But between digital and earlier celluloid, it is even less. Nonetheless, you still need to know basically the camera, lens, light—all of that. But that is an awareness which will make an actor express himself better in front of the mechanical eye. But I do remember that much can happen at the edit table. Say, for example, within a shot, there is a dull moment for an actor followed by a moment where he gives a sensitive expression. If the editor cuts out that delicate acting moment, the entire shot may become dull and the acting may look quite placid as well. An actor is less privileged in cinema than in theatre.'

***

To describe the job of acting, Soumitra provided several analogies at several points in time. He would draw inspiration from Abanindranath Tagore's explanation when he mentioned that a good actor is like the flight of a bird, effortless, smooth and silent. He differentiated this with a lesser actor whose acting resembles an airplane. The plane flies, like the bird, but it makes a lot of noise and is unable to conceal the techniques of flying. At other times, Soumitra would clarify that in any example of superlative art form, technique and emotion are not separate things, because we will never say a great horse but a lousy jockey. They both become one in pursuit of excellence.

The Bengali film industry, in spite of its artistic quality and contribution, has mostly been a limited one in terms of commerce for the past five decades. Unfortunately, since the late '70s, mainstream commercial Bengali cinema looked towards Hindi and South Indian films for inspiration and source of content. Being a professional, Soumitra had to adjust his acting ideals and sensitivities to continue being relevant. As he moulded himself, he carved a niche for himself in the process as well, creating a character pattern of the Bengali, educated, middle-class elderly.

Yet, as the remunerations in the Bengali industry continued to be ridiculous as compared to Hindi or South Indian films, Soumitra had to work endlessly in a number of shoddy films just to earn his living. With such a barrage of insensitive and meaningless work, how could he still maintain his freshness to sparkle in that one-off exceptional film that came his way? There was no doubt that even in the last three decades of his film acting, he could deliver at least two to three memorable performances in each of them, those that would have been coveted by the best in the industry.

Soumitra elucidated this dichotomy with a brilliant analogy again. He narrated how, in his boyhood days, he would see small boats being submerged in water when not in use. Then, as the monsoon rain swelled the rivers and overflowed the banks, these boats were brought up and used. A true actor's sensitivities are also like these small boats, which he may immerse deep under his senses. When the appropriate role demands, the practiced actor will be able to unravel the finer pathos in his deliverance.

The key to this probably lies in the fact that Soumitra was

a perennially inquisitive person whose focus of interest was not only in nature around him but also the human beings he met on his journey. Long before he became an actor, Soumitra's lust for life drove him to analyse people he would observe on the streets—why a man was walking in a particular way, what was his home like, who all were there in his family, how was his bathroom or kitchen, his relation with his wife or girlfriend, so on and so forth. No doubt he was thoroughly influenced by Stanislavski's methods of preparation and also Pudovkin's prescriptions for detailed research for an actor.

From early on, Soumitra tried to approach a character from the perspectives of psychology and character traits. This included the physical attributes of the character, the potential dressing styles along with colour schemes, the probable make-up required including hair, beard, moustache. As he started with the exterior manifestations of a character, the inner dynamics automatically started gushing out. That is why, in most of his memorable performances, he did not merely act out a character of the script with his expertise. Rather, he breathed life into the characters as complete human beings based on his understanding and curiosity as an artist of the highest order.

This curiosity and restlessness to express and be connected with the higher faculties of consciousness drove him to try new forms, to venture out of the narrow-minded existence of parochial back-thumping. In the late '70s, he voice-acted the role of Amit in Tagore's *Sesher Kabita* as an audio drama. It became so popular that it had to be performed several times, recorded as a cassette for sale eventually and then as a very popular audio CD. When the Calcutta unit of Doordarshan started in the mid-'70s, Soumitra was once again one of the frontrunners to understand the importance of the medium.

In those days of black-and-white projection, Soumitra acted in Tagore's *Malancha*, one of the earliest productions of Doordarshan. When television serials commenced in the mid-'80s, Soumitra soon balanced his time between theatre, cinema and television by engaging in serials including Saratchandra's immensely popular *Dena Paona*, Badal Sarkar's comedy *Solution X* and Tarashankar Banerjee's epic, *Arogya Niketan*. In parallel, he also wrote, directed and acted in *Mahasindhur Opar Hotey* as a Bengali teleplay for Doordarshan in 1989. With the advent and rapid success of mega serials since the late '90s, Soumitra became less frequent, unable to provide dedicated time for Doordarshan and was thoroughly disgusted by the general low standards of production.

It was in Doordarshan that Soumitra acted as Feluda for the two productions, *Golokdham Rahasya* and *Ghurghutiyar Ghatana*, in 1992. Directed by Bibhas Chakraborty, Soumitra was reluctant to play the iconic character which he had made immortal almost two decades back. A wise Soumitra understood that his age wouldn't befit Felu, who was an icon of the youth. Also, both the stories were without Jatayu, Feluda's equally popular sidekick made a legend by Santosh Dutta on-screen.

After Dutta's death, Ray himself decided never to make another film of the sleuth just because there wouldn't be a matching Jatayu. A persistent Chakraborty persuaded Ray, who finally convinced Soumitra that if anyone had to play the role, it had to be him. Soumitra didn't like either of the two versions. Later, Ray's son Sandip made a number of films featuring Feluda, first for television and then as feature films, with Sabyasachi Chakraborty playing the sleuth in a majority of them.

However, apart from the two feature films, *Sonar Kella* and *Joy Baba Felunath*, Satyajit Ray and Soumitra Chatterjee were involved in a couple of other Feluda projects as well. *Baksho Rahasya* and *Gonsaipur Sargaram* were two stories which were scripted by Sandip for radio plays back in 1984. Initially, instead of Soumitra, a younger Santu Mukherjee was commissioned to voice Feluda. The rumour so went that after the broadcast of the first fifteen-minute instalment of the play in All India Radio's Vividh Bharati programme, such was the furore over Mukherjee giving voice to Feluda that Ray had to bring in Soumitra Chatterjee, Santosh Dutta and Siddhartha Chatterjee—the original trio of the film versions. Ray himself was probably not very happy with the initial performance and the recording was made all over again, this time with the original—and more popular—cast.

Soumitra's identification with Feluda was so complete that a few years later, when Sandip directed a Hindi version of *Joto Kando Kathmandu-te* as *Kissa Kathmandu Mein* in 1986-87 as part of the television series *Satyajit Ray Presents* for DD National, Ray was apprehensive of Shashi Kapoor playing the detective. A visibly plump Kapoor was understandably not accepted by Bengalis worldwide. To many, for whom Feluda represents a quintessential Bengali who relies more on his intellect and intelligence than his physical strength and mechanical aids, Soumitra is till today the most authentic Feluda who has ever graced the silver screen.

EIGHT

The King

On 12 September 2013, an exhibition of Soumitra Chatterjee's paintings commenced at the Indian Council for Cultural Relations (ICCR), Calcutta. The exhibition that continued for a week was inaugurated by filmmaker Mrinal Sen and the paintings were selected by veteran artist and a longtime friend of Soumitra, Rabin Mondal. For the general public, it was discovering a hitherto unknown side of Soumitra's creativity. People close to him and those who were involved in theatre or cinema alongside him had known of Soumitra's scribbles and doodles. Most of these were made on expired invitation cards or other pieces of papers.

Like his mentor Ray, Soumitra's working theatre script used to be replete with drawings and sketches—of sets and of different characters. Later, filmmaker Atanu Ghosh told me that at the time of the first script-reading session of his films that cast Soumitra, the actor would take a piece of paper and start doodling on it as Ghosh kept on reading. Once the reading was over, Soumitra would show the sketch to Ghosh, which was his idea of the character by listening to the script. Atanu Ghosh found them remarkably close to his mental image of the characters, almost always.

Soumitra had always maintained, even after the exhibition, that painting and sketching were his spare time activities, more for fun than a serious vocation. Often, during long breaks between shooting schedules or when work had to be cancelled for unavoidable reasons, Soumitra would bring out his notebook. Even at times of mental crises or personal depressions, when he was not willing to surrender his feelings to his more faithful poetry, he would vent out on the empty paper—not with words but in lines. Only in the last few years of his life, after the exhibition, did he take painting and drawing more seriously, experimenting with a few styles and media and, more importantly, devoting conscious time to it.

In his early youth in Howrah, he was a follower, in the literal sense, of Rabin Mondal. Soumitra watched Mondal sketch Mahatma Gandhi delivering a speech from a podium on one of many occasions when he accompanied Mondal. None of Soumitra's immediate family was a painter. But, like in many educated and enlightened middle-class Bengali families, the Chatterjees subscribed to monthly literary magazines, such as *Prabasi* and *Bharatbarsha*. These magazines used to carry artworks of prominent artists regularly. It was here that Soumitra started getting exposed to the paintings of Gaganendranath Tagore, Abanindranath Tagore, Nandalal Bose, Hemen Majumdar and others.

There was another direct influence apart from Rabin Mondal. Chaitanyadeb Chatterjee was an immediate disciple of Abanindranath Tagore and a proponent of the Bengal School of Art who became quite famous with his 'Ghat Series' of paintings on life around the banks of the Ganga. Chaitanyadeb's wife was Soumitra's distant cousin and both their sons—Buddhadeb and Shukdeb—were older than Soumitra. Soumitra was very fond of these two older nephews of his and used to regularly visit their home at Bhadrakali, on the Grand Trunk Road.

Both brothers learnt drawing from their father and both of them, primarily Shukdeb, guided Soumitra in sketching. Much later, Chaitanyadeb quit his earlier style of painting and worked on forms and figures interspersed with a dense mesh of lines and criss-crossing over his writings. He might have been influenced by Rabindranath Tagore's own form of doodling and dense pen strokes on written words. This form influenced Soumitra deeply.

Watching Chaitanyadeb's works and also Rabindranath's helped him develop a similar style. Though he painted landscapes, he picked up acrylic instead of watercolour much later. After the success of the exhibition, he never gave up this style of criss-crossing and mixing text with lines.

A close look at Soumitra's artwork will reveal that a majority are faces and profiles. His long stint of being an actor definitely influenced his style and genre of painting in terms of finding the human face as the most revealing aspect to sketch. Acclaimed painter Jogen Chowdhury analysed his work thus: 'Soumitra-da's creations are not a result of formal training in the field of art; rather, they are a result of a spontaneous outburst of his multifaceted creativity. His artworks consist of beautiful patterns that have resulted from dense lines and criss-crosses in ink, merging with a vast range of colours. His paintings contain faces and expressions of individuals who have touched his life in some way or the other. This is of course very natural ... Careful introspection of Soumitra-da's artworks gives us a fascinating insight into the artist's personality.

'His creations reflect the vast range of thoughts that wander through his mind; creations depicting facial expressions, human characters, female figures, landscapes, strange animals—all formed by the extraordinary amalgamation of dark, dense lines and criss-crosses ... Through his paintings, we are able to discover an entirely new facet of Soumitra Chatterjee. His

Painter Jogen Chowdhury along with Soumitra at the latter's exhibition 'Forms Within'
(Photo Credit: Jyotirmoy Bhattacharya)

paintings provide us with an insight into the artist's innermost thoughts, an insight into the alternate shadows of hope and despair that traverse his mind, a glimpse of the subtle shades of joy and sorrow that fill his heart.'*

After the Calcutta exhibition, Soumitra's paintings travelled west; there were a couple of subsequent ones in Baroda and Ahmedabad. In both places, his paintings were appreciated by leading Indian painters including K.G. Subramanyan and Manu Parekh. Perhaps the finest analysis of his works came from his childhood friend and guide, Rabin Mondal: 'Some of his works deserve a special mention as they are of superlative quality ... His use of colours while creating images lends them a certain mysterious value ... The strokes have a lyrical quality in them ... it would not be irrelevant to mention that Soumitra has left an unparalleled footprint in the fields of cinema and theatre, and he definitely has our eager attention as he dabbles with the field of art.'†

***

Soumitra was fond of reiterating how he kept on egging himself to carry on till he was eighty-five, how each day of living needed to be meaningful. Akira Kurosawa, the great Japanese director, happened to be Soumitra's most favourite film director. In repeated discussions, he mentioned Kurosawa to be the 'Shakespeare of cinema'. He explained that Kurosawa,

---

* *Forms Within: Soumitra Chatterjee*, Art Alinda, 2013.
† Ibid.

according to him, had the most variations of themes—from the likes of *Lower Depths* to *Seven Samurai*, *High and Low* to *Red Beard* and then *Dreams* or *Madadayo*. It was Kurosawa's meaningful observation about the varied aspects of life including the struggles within the classes and the violence that erupts from the clashes that drew Soumitra to Kurosawa's body of work.

An ardent admirer of Satyajit Ray (whom Kurosawa admired a lot as well), Soumitra realized that Ray's social positioning didn't allow him to capture the struggles and tribulations of the lower strata of society. The seedy side of life, the vigour, violence, antagonism and deceit that were rooted in Shakespeare's plays and in Kurosawa's adaptations, *Throne of Blood* (*Macbeth*) and *Ran* (*King* Lear), were not Ray's cinematic vision, which was focussed more on the delicate aspects of human existence.

In a poem titled 'Birthday', Soumitra paid tribute to Akira Kurosawa. The poem was inspired by Kurosawa's last film, *Madadayo*, meaning 'Not Yet'. A contemplative film about death and aging, it ultimately celebrates life and, more importantly, living.

> *He may again receive news of a death today,*
> *At his age, turning sixty—this is regular,*
> *One after another near ones part away leaving him alone,*
> *Death comes an inch nearer, walks alongside, yet*
> *No one thinks ever the man reached a ripe age—*
> *Light dyed hair, upright figure—slim,*
> *Sparkling healthy teeth, a lovely smile,*
> *Who will ever think of death walking alongside him?*

No one tells him, or will ever, but he knows the best—
the burning, loss, fatigue and sorrows engulfing him in this age.

He may receive news of death even today,
A companion in this game, a partner, rather,
Calling out to him each time—'Ready?'
He frantically wriggles away—'No, not yet, not now.'

The game of hide-and-seek goes on as life turns sixty,
Even when the body looks healthy,
this game doesn't stop, repeats—
Does death blow through his light hair—
A passing breeze whispering to him, 'Ready?'

He then looks up at the sky
forgetting the game of fatigue, new clouds up there
A change of season garnishing life.*

Soumitra's acting in theatre took a definitive turn with his 2006 production, *Homapakhi*. Written by Amit Ranjan Biswas, a neuropsychiatrist based in the UK, this was one of Soumitra's rare productions where he hadn't written the play himself. The only notable one before *Homapakhi* was Manoj Mitra's *Darpane Sarat Sashi*, apart from Girish Ghosh's *Bilwamangal Thakur*. A popular play with repeat performances for years, Soumitra followed *Homapakhi* with *Atmakatha* (original play by Mahesh Elkunchwar).

In most of his critically acclaimed plays till then, Soumitra had acted in characters far removed from the class and time of

---

* Soumitra Chatterjee, *Walking through the Mist*, Tr.: Amitava Nag, Dhauli Books, 2020, pp. 23-24.

his own. With *Homapakhi*, for the first time he was depicting a character, a retired professor, who was more of an extension of the profile he had perfected on-screen for the past two decades or so. The middle-class, intelligent, educated 'bhadralok', which he typified on-screen, was translated on stage first with *Homapakhi* and then in *Atmakatha*.

Soumitra with co-actors Poulami Chatterjee and Lily Chakraborty in *Atmakatha*
(Photo Credit: Bilu Dutta)

In *Atmakatha*, for example, Soumitra played a septuagenarian writer Subhankar, who is looking back at his life in the process of writing an autobiography. He is helped by Prajna, a young research scholar who is a big admirer of Subhankar. Soumitra brings in strains of Sashi Bhushan from *Dekha* but extends it more in the philosophical exploration of a creative mind. The play with three physical sections on the stage moves back and forth at different time levels as Subhankar travels in time looking back at his life and the injustices done to his wife and her sister, with whom he had a relationship.

Like his evolved cinematic acting style, Soumitra adopted a very minimalistic expressive approach in both these plays, yet bringing out the fine emotional conflicts of the characters. In *Homapakhi*, the problems were of bipolar mood swings and depressions and forgetfulness. In *Atmakatha*, on the contrary, the memories were too vivid.

Atmakatha was first performed in July 2008. The next year, between 9 and 28 May, Soumitra wrote *Tritiyo Anko, Atoeb*, a name he borrowed from his favourite poet, Jibanananda Das's poem, 'Uttarprabesh' written in 1948. It was Soumitra's one and only consciously autobiographical attempt, although throughout his life he had criticized biographical attempts with mordant wit. However, in retrospect, *Tritiyo Anko, Atoeb* is a very pertinent successor of *Atmakatha*.

Soumitra here was more contained, his performance more minimalistic and subtle as he was playing himself, the actor and celebrity, 'Soumitra Chatterjee'. Soumitra developed severe heart ailments in 2007 and by late 2008, he was diagnosed with prostate cancer. His treatment started in Calcutta but he had to travel to England for expert advice and further therapy. The forced break in England enabled him to watch a number of films.

When I asked him in one of my earlier conversations if he had been his own propagandist in this play, Soumitra opposed the idea. To him, it was more of an experiment with the structure of the play and the form of the content. The form, he believed, could only be tried if he put himself under the radar instead of anyone else, to avoid controversies. While in England, he watched Simon Gray and Hugh Whitemore's play, *The Last Cigarette*, based on Simon Gray's memoir, *The Smoking Diaries*. In the play, three characters played Gray to depict a part of his life.

Soumitra drew his inspiration from it. 'I followed the same format though the story, culture and everything were different. When I am no longer alive, someone else can do the role but since I am available now, I decided to play myself, taking two of my most dependable and close actors—Dwijen Banerjee and Poulami Chatterjee. The decision to make it autobiographical was a conscious one. This type of theatre has never been done in our country. You may ask why not one character but three. The answer to that is with one character, it would have been very monotonous. Also, one actor acting out the different interactions with different people would have been less refreshing. At my age, I was keen to contemplate how a person faces old age, illness and how he wants to welcome the eventual reality, death—it is my view of my last days in the mould of an autobiography.'*

---

* Amitava Nag, *Beyond Apu: 20 Favourite Film Roles of Soumitra Chatterjee*, HarperCollins Publishers India, 2016, pp. 148-149.

The play had mixed reactions from the public. The first half was entertaining, inspirational at times with the audience getting a feel of Soumitra's persona, the turbulence of youth, his anxieties and concerns. More importantly, it was the memories that nurtured a creative mind, unfurled its possibilities and guided it to attain greater heights. The third act overflowed with the minutest details of his medical history, the tests and investigations, a virulent monotony of a tired mind seeking attention. A section of the audience found it too much to bear, because these details made them sad for a personality who had influenced the Bengali psyche for over half a century.

More importantly, they found it irrelevant to listen to the long list of ailments and the associated hazards that Soumitra Chatterjee had to endure. The play ends with Soumitra shrugging off these depressive traits and looking at death not as an end but as a celebration of a life well lived. To this audience, the final prophetic sermon was lost—they were too dispirited already or bored anyway to take home Soumitra's message about being strong in the face of loss.

Like Subhankar in *Atmakatha*, 'Soumitra Chatterjee' in *Tritiyo Anko, Atoeb* was also sketched out in an unforgiving tone. Soumitra, the playwright, had always been merciless in self-critique. In *Rajkumar*, written three decades back, he was equally unforgiving, ruthless and uncompromising. In *Tritiyo Anko, Atoeb* as well, Soumitra was fierce and candid with a generous dose of dark humour addressed to the self.

The first scene of the second act of the play commenced with recollections about his mother. Two years hence, just before the second act at the break, Soumitra came to know that his mother passed away at the age of ninety-seven. She had been quite critical for a few days before that. It was very emotional for Soumitra but being a professional actor, he had to make sure that sentiments didn't get the better of him.

Soumitra launched *Tritiyo Anko, Atoeb* as a new play before his seventy-fifth birthday, on 12 January 2010, shortly after he had recovered enough, both mentally as well as physically, to be back in action. The same year, on 14 November in Minerva Theatre, Soumitra Chatterjee appeared on stage as King Lear.

***

Soumitra had always dreamt and wished to play a Shakespearean character on-screen. He was fascinated by *Hamlet* and nourished a desire to play the prince of Denmark for many years. As he grew old, he understood that it would be physically difficult for him to act as Hamlet anymore.

Minerva Repertory Theatre was a government organization formed to produce quality theatre supported by the state government. The repertory had salaried professionals as actors and technicians. It started in July 2010 and for their first production, they invited Soumitra Chatterjee to act and direct a play for them.

Soumitra informed the officials that he would be interested in doing *King Lear*, but he would not wish to take the load of directing such a huge project. It was Soumitra who suggested that the Minerva officials contact noted film and theatre director, Suman Mukherjee, to direct the play for the repertory. Suman quite obviously felt it was a great honour for him to direct Soumitra on stage.

Earlier, in Catherine Berge's compassionate documentary on Soumitra, *Gaach*, there were snippets of the play that the thespian had acted along with Rabi Ghosh playing the Fool. That had however increased our thirst to watch Soumitra play Lear in a full-fledged play. *Raja Lear* was set up with a grand design and interesting use of architectural levels and light projections. The background score was quite dramatic, befitting the epic saga. Acting is very important in this type of play which relies a lot on lengthy dialogues and in being predominantly verbose to carry forward the narrative.

Soumitra feared having problems with remembering his lines even though he otherwise had an almost phenomenal memory. He would write the entire script from memory a couple of times just to ensure that he didn't forget anything. Unlike *Atmakatha* and *Tritiyo Anko, Atoeb*, Soumitra had to prepare more intensely, more deeply, for Lear. This was a bigger-than-life character, a dream one, and Soumitra left no stone unturned in preparing himself for Lear. He would draw sketches of Lear in different moods and compose poems on the king and the tragic events that unfold with the progression of the play. At times, he would still forget lines on stage, but never faltered. Such was his grasp of the Bengali language that he could carry on without the audience finding out.

Raja Lear had a multi-layered stage and Soumitra had to climb up and down, move around, run, when the king turned mad. There was a scene when the second daughter throws him out of the house and the angry king would trip on the stage out of dizziness and frustration. Every time that scene was played out, Soumitra would deliver it with such authentic physicality that the audience would gasp with concern and worry. Soumitra's health problems were well known by then and the viewers were genuinely worried. With every performance, Soumitra would make it look a little more precarious, enjoying the sound of a collective gasp from his spectators.

In an article, Suman Mukherjee reminisced about Soumitra's dedication and approach to the character. 'He'd arrive three hours before each performance, after doing his make-up, changing into his costume, 15-20 minutes before the play, he'd go sit in the background darkness, alone, contemplative. The first day when I went to shake his hands to wish him good luck, he said, „ *Eyi Suman, parbo toh, hobe toh* (Will I be able to do it)?„ He was never complacent, never overconfident. That uncertainty is an artist's real, true spirit.

'In spite of being a long-standing successful thespian, he always had that sense of uncertainty of creativity. Lear was him, he got personally attached to the character. Every day, after the performance, he'd say, „ I feel completely blank.„ Lear dies at the end, and after he dies, there are almost six-seven minutes of the play remaining before the curtain comes down. He'd always say, „ In those moments, while lying there on the stage floor, I feel that I'm hanging in some strange place, I know not what that is.„ Since it was his dream role, he gave everything possible into the making of the character.'*

---

* Suman Mukherjee, 'If he was on the stage, you'd not look at anybody else', *The Indian Express*, 21 November 2020, accessed on 6 June 2021, https://indianexpress.com/article/lifestyle/art-and-culture/soumitra-chatterjee-death-passing-theatre-films-movies-suman-mukhopadhyay-7058877/

Soumitra as Lear in the play *Raja Lear*
(Photo Credit: Minerva Repertory Theatre
and Suman Mukherjee)

Raja Lear was the biggest theatre phenomenon for decades that preceded it. It became so popular that tickets would be sold out in no time. The production was taken out of Minerva, because it had a capacity of less than five hundred seats. Subsequent performances happened at bigger auditoriums like Rabindra Sadan, Girish Mancha and Madhusudan Mancha. Within a few performances, *Raja Lear* achieved an iconic status. At a time when even the better-run Bengali theatre productions had a ticket price of Rs 100 to Rs 150, the same for *Raja Lear* soared to a record Rs 500 in 2010-11.

The main attraction of the play was Soumitra. He was on stage for more than two hours in a play close to three hours. The physical acting was stupendous. There was the violent impetus, the blind swagger against any voice that was not relenting, the royal impatience—King Lear was embodied in flesh and soul. The original play and this adaptation as well successfully vacillated between the ebb and tide of emotions, embedded with typical Machiavellian deceit and manipulations. He literally lived the transformation from a king of England to pauper at heart, confronted by his two cold-blooded elder daughters. His longing for being loved and for being cradled by his daughters made the Fool jibe at him—'...he has made his daughters his mothers.' The father's innate love and fervour makes Lear endearingly human—and not just a king. Soumitra's pathos, the anxiety, the wounded father, was as much the king as any Bengali father. In deft touches, he played to the heart, connecting to the soul of the audience distressed at the plight of a battered father.

Soumitra lived Lear on stage, fumbling, childish and at times lamenting for not having stripped his royal overcoat earlier. In a way, Soumitra roped in the audience with him; Lear left the mortal structure, reverberated in the auditorium and then inhabited the soul of every member of the audience. When he murmured to his youngest daughter, Cordelia, 'Won't you stay back just a while more, dear?', Soumitra took our breath away for the tragedy of life, for Lear and his three daughters, but more for the absurd nothingness of our mundane lives.

Once, after one of Lear's performances, I asked whose influence he had on him, if any, in depicting this role. Soumitra closed his eyes, diving into his mind, and then told me, 'I wanted to do something which probably will give you an idea of what Sisir Kumar would have done, had he done it.' Modest at heart, he quickly added that he couldn't achieve all of it. I reminded him then that those who were privileged to watch Sisir Kumar on stage and him playing Neelkantha vouched for the lineage. But I agreed; Soumitra's Lear was so big that it deserves a separate mention as an independent chapter in the history of post-independent Indian dramatic performances.

Despite the accolades, exciting reviews and audience adoration, *Raja Lear* ran into issues from the very beginning. Soumitra's association with Minerva Repertory and Suman's involvement germinated in the CPI(M) era when the play started its performances. Suman himself was not a very favoured intellectual during the CPI(M) rule and his 2005 film *Herbert* ran into all sorts of trouble under the Left government for ultra-Left leanings.

Within the inner circles of the West Bengal government during that time, he was identified as a well-wisher of the opposition, the Trinamool Congress (TMC) party and Mamata Banerjee, its supremo. The TMC came to power in 2011 after thirty-four years of Left regime in West Bengal.

Soon after, the new government apparently reviewed the commercial viability of *Raja Lear* and deemed it unfit for continuation. The grapevine had it that the new rulers didn't approve of Soumitra's association with Minerva Repertory (it being a government organization) due to his much-touted sympathy for the earlier administration. Spread between two governments and attacked by both regimes for non-theatrical reasons, *Raja Lear* was stopped and revived on several occasions, with gaps of over six months at times.

All this left everyone bitter, including Soumitra, who had been displeased with the functioning of the repertory even before the first stage performance. His *Gadya Sangraha, Volume 2* includes a short note from his diary written on 19 October 2010 (less than a month from *Raja Lear*'s first performance) and probably edited and modified on 1 August 2016 before it was handed over to the publisher. It was the last essay of the volume and there are no guesses to the insurmountable pain Soumitra bore in his heart in those six years as he witnessed the vested interests that derailed the possibilities of a resurrection of Bengali theatre and the general listlessness around him.

It details the meagre monetary emoluments that Soumitra was offered a day before the rehearsals started, by which time, he had already committed based on verbal assurances and letting go his other assignments in cinema and advertisements. Soumitra felt he was tricked into playing the role in spite of all his excitement and eagerness to enact Lear. He explains how he compromised his remuneration while acting in commercial theatre in the '80s and '90s with the zeal to act in front of a packed audience in a set-up which was dwindling already. But a government-backed repertory could have done better in attracting sponsors post 2010.

In an aggrieved tone, Soumitra concludes, 'My acting in theatre is a saga of deprivation. That is why I think at times, why should I continue acting in theatre? That is why even though the thought of not acting any more swayed like a cry near my throat, I could never spell it out. In the past fifty-two years of my professional acting career, so many people thanked me for my work—terminally ill patients or mentally deranged individuals came up to me and showed their gratitude, told me how my work inspired them to live on—those faces, thousands of them, resurface in my mind. Then I realize in this third world, there are so many things which don't get their due. Maybe it is the same with me as well.'*

Even years after Soumitra Chatterjee stopped playing Lear on stage, in many intimate discussions with friends, he would bring up why Lear's tragedy was universally primal, stirring infinite melancholy, dejection and sorrow. In 2019, he was reading *1606: Shakespeare and the Year of Lear* and then *1599: A Year in the Life of William Shakespeare*. In every subsequent discussion, he would discuss Shakespeare, that how mesmerized he was thinking that when *Othello* and *Hamlet* were already written, and he was probably mulling on *Macbeth*, Shakespeare could write *King Lear* as an intermediate piece. In his later years, Soumitra just breathed Shakespeare, reading everything that he could lay his hands on. To understand Soumitra Chatterjee, we need to appreciate this curious mind and this homework which he did while approaching some of his most iconic characters.

At the far end of his career, Soumitra Chatterjee got a chance to play a Shakespearean character. To him, the ultimate hallmark of a great acting piece was in bringing Shakespeare

---

* Soumitra Chatterjee, *Gadya Sangraha*, Volume 2, Dey's Publishing, 2016, p.893—translated by the author.

to life. There was nothing bigger or better than that on stage. He continued to act in other plays subsequently, launched a few new ones, acted in some of them as well. But the golden moment of Soumitra's acting laurels in theatre would be when after three hours on stage, the curtains would rise and he would bow down to his captive audience.

Neither Lear nor Shakespeare ever left Soumitra Chatterjee. Even during those gaps in performance, Soumitra remained Bengali theatre's undisputed monarch. A king will always remain a king—either on the throne or in exile.

NINE

Bela Seshe

Soumitra directed and acted in *Bidehi* way back in 1972 as one of Abhinetri Sangha's productions. He translated the play almost literally, unlike most of his later ones, from Henrik Ibsen's *Ghosts*. At that time, Soumitra played the lead character of Oswald Alving with Nilima Das playing his mother, Mrs Alving. Precisely four decades hence, Soumitra took up *Bidehi* again in 2012 and retranslated it. When asked why he translated *Ghosts* instead of transcreating it to Bengali soil like his other plays, Soumitra once explained, 'I somehow felt that an adaptation would be difficult because the social and cultural differences are too vivid. I felt that an adaptation will not be that convincing. There is no place in India where a six-month-long winter will put people into complete isolation. The psychology of the characters stems from that and I will never be able to bring that out in a Bengali context.

'If I have to make an adaptation, I will have to introduce

Captain Alving as a character with less moral values due to other reasons than those expressed in the original play. But then again, that Oswald is also a victim of similar circumstances will be difficult to establish. In addition, the setting has a very fundamental Christian context. Pastor Manders is a family friend and one with whom Mrs Alving was involved at a time. In the Indian context, where will you find a noble lady being friends with a priest and also, the whole concept of confession isn't there in our religion. In essence, for an adaptation, I will then need to change the profiles of almost all the five characters, which I felt will be very impertinent.'

However, several hurdles kept *Bidehi* from being staged immediately. Finally, it was, after four years, on 2 November 2016 at 6:30 pm at the Academy of Fine Arts. The posters of *Bidehi* proudly proclaimed 'Three generations on stage'. Soumitra confessed to me that he thought of the retranslation with a wish to direct his grandson Ronodeep Bose as Oswald, the hero he used to play forty years back. Ronodeep was a musician and had already started making his entry into Bengali cinema with *Dutta Vs Dutta*, *Kshoto*, *Egaro* and others. His acting talent was never questioned although his focus seemed wavering.

From the time of retranslation till the actual production, Soumitra found himself unable to direct a new play as the physical strain was too much for him. He however played Engstrand with restrained brilliance. Poulami, Soumitra's daughter, was the creative director of the theatre group, Shyambajar Mukhomukhi, which agreed to produce *Bidehi*. Poulami was remaking Soumitra's own *Phera* after several decades, apart from playing the character of Mrs Alving and was too busy to direct *Bidehi*. Noted theatre personality Kaushik Sen came onboard as director.

The issues of promiscuity, incest and immorality as appearing in *Bidehi*, which seemed taboo in the nineteenth century, have eased over time. What still resonate however are the questions of euthanasia, hypocrisy, the role of women as providers yet sufferers and, most importantly, the degenerating values of family life. Watching three generations of Soumitra, Poulami and Ronodeep on stage ensured that *Bidehi* became a big hit right from its premiere. Its success rode on astute direction, an inspiring set and marvellous acting from the entire cast, particularly Poulami.

Just when everyone involved with *Bidehi* started settling down to bask in its triumph, in less than six months, tragedy rocked Soumitra's life and crippled the production of *Bidehi* forever. On the fateful night of 30 March 2017, rather the wee hours of the 31st, Ronodeep met with a severe accident while riding a motorcycle. Suffering from an extremely critical head injury, Rono, as he was fondly referred to, slipped into a deep coma for months on end. Brain surgeries, several therapies, life-saving drug treatments and five years later, he is on the way to recovery, though it will be a long walk back to a semblance of his previous life.

Ronodeep's catastrophe pushed Soumitra to a state of deep anguish, restlessness and despair. An otherwise orderly man, Soumitra could tame his inner turmoil every time previously. But this time, it was almost beyond repair. He stopped his paintings and scribblings; poetry refused to flow with the fluency it had before. Theatre shows were postponed, film shootings were in disarray. The treatment was expensive. He needed more work, along with Poulami. To me and to most other friends, he always confessed that his biggest nightmare since then was to leave at a time when his family needed him the most—psychologically and also financially.

Soumitra's health condition remained a concern. This despite a strict medical vigil and restrictions to remain fit for work. At least two of them were bothersome—malignancy and a susceptible respiratory tract problem. In the medical tour of England in the last decade, it was decided that Soumitra, given his age, would not go for surgery. Nonetheless, the knowledge of a silent slayer residing in the body was enough for Soumitra to take stock of unresolved things. It was with this urgency that he engaged more and more with painting, stopped briefly due to Rono's condition.

It was the second assassin which landed Soumitra in the hospital, for the penultimate time, on 14 August 2019 after he complained of breathing problems. Admitted to the intensive care unit, his vitals were soon restored and he returned home after a week with recommended rest of three more weeks. The initial problems were overcome in a day or so but he was kept on observation for the rest of the week before being discharged. It was during this idle phase in the hospital that his scribbles were more about loneliness and death—one in particular about the bank of a river with a boat waiting to leave the shores as an ambulance returns. He also wrote soliloquies about his responsibilities, fears and wishes to work till his end.

***

Soumitra dabbled in several artforms throughout his life. But with age, as his film acting challenges reduced (though the number of films with diminishing acting scope increased), writing and directing plays swelled since the '90s. Writing poems and essays were a constant but since the '90s, he started publishing anthologies more often. As early as 1993, his *Srestha Kabita* (Best Verses) was published by Dey's Publishing. Soumitra continued experimenting with poetic forms, bringing out a couple of limerick collections in 1996 and 1999 apart from thirteen books of poems since *Srestha Kabita* was published. Of these, in the last decade, he had one anthology of poems almost every alternate year. He was writing a lot, breaking his older structures and trying out newer roads.

At the twilight of his acting career, two films stand out again in his oeuvre, one in particular for significantly breaking his own mannerisms in older roles. One of this was *Bela Seshe* by the director duo of Nandita Roy and Shiboprosad Mukherjee. The directors had already made a few 'social' films, as they are referred to, upholding strong family values and moral codes. Based on the strength, weaknesses and love of a joint-family setting that prevents the breakdown of the marriage of an elderly couple, the film hit the right chord with the general audience.

It was the biggest hit in Bengali cinema for years, running at a stretch of more than two hundred days in multiplexes and single-screen halls. The film was released nationally and even in the UK, the US, Singapore and also Bangladesh. The success of the film resulted in a spin-off titled *Bela Shuru*. Soumitra was part of it as well and the film was slated to be released in 2020, which was cancelled due to the COVID pandemic.

Soumitra relished the success of *Bela Seshe*. He always insisted that, being a professional actor, his commitment had always been to cinema and the films he was associated with. His personal preferences in judging art were never a hindrance in such acceptances. Rather, he would jokingly narrate how he became quite popular among the non-Bengali-speaking audience once again with *Bela Seshe*. In one particular instance, I found a few children going up to him and asking for autographs. Thinking that they might have watched Soumitra's iconic Feluda, they suddenly proved both of us wrong by calling out in glee, '*Bela Seshe*-r dadu'.

Soumitra instantaneously winked at me. 'Don't be disappointed. I represent all the films I made.' After *Bela Seshe*, Soumitra was repeated twice in subsequent years by the same director duo, in *Praktan* and *Posto*. Both films had golden runs at the box office.

The other film which was indeed path-breaking in terms of Soumitra's portrayal was Atanu Ghosh's *Mayurakshi*. Soumitra had already acted in a few telefilms of Atanu earlier; in his first feature *Anghsumaner Chhobi* in 2009 and then playing the same older benevolent character he had played so many times with perfection in *Rupkatha Noy* in 2013. In *Mayurakshi*, four years down the time, Soumitra portrayed Sushobhan, a retired professor of history, who is suffering from age-related neurological problems, including dementia and cognitive dysfunction.

In most of the current films, Soumitra mostly portrayed central characters who have a sophisticated urbaneness in them. Middle-class, educated, most importantly alert and vibrant—an

Soumitra with Prasenjit in Atanu Ghosh's *Mayurakshi*
(Photo Credit: Atanu Ghosh)

image that was surreptitiously associated with Soumitra. He and the characters he acted mingled into a profile of the conscience, a guardian of the Bengali milieu. The character of Sushobhan is so refreshingly different because of his vulnerability. Sushobhan, due to his ailments, is forgetful, unmindful, like an errant child who neglects his homework halfway. In many adroit moments, he evoked in the audience the pathos and love for their prized elderly parents, in memory or in life.

Soumitra wanted to work till his very last days. Even in the last five years of his life, beyond eighty, he was a busy actor. His role as a manipulative old man with a seductive young wife in Sujoy Ghosh's short film *Ahalya* was the talk of the town in 2015. Then again, the old patriarch that he essayed in Suman Ghosh's *Basu Poribar* and Anik Dutta's *Borunbabur Bondhu* in 2018 and 2020 respectively, secured his position once more as an almost irreplaceable character actor of the decade. Probably, this profile as an upright, yet benevolent and humble patriarch for whom there will be audience sympathy right from the start (unlike Chhabi Biswas, whose type was to be more wary of than loved) will no longer be seen on-screen. There will be different profiles of the old henceforth on the Bengali screen, not the one that Soumitra portrayed with elegance and finesse.

After he passed away, there were more than ten films in different phases of making, and several waiting to be released. Parambrata Chatterjee's *Abhijan*, a biopic on him, is one such. He finally permitted a biopic on him with Jissu Sengupta playing his younger days and he himself as the octogenarian. He was even involved in a documentary on himself which aspired to hold his multifaceted persona in the light of conversations with several eminent artists—of theatre, cinema, literature and painting. It was during the shooting of this documentary that he contracted the deadly COVID virus, got admitted to a private hospital on 6 October 2020 and finally passed away on 15 November 2020 after a long and grim battle.

During this period, when he was battling for life in the hospital, Bengalis all over the world were pensive, distraught, agitated, sad. They found it difficult to channelize their emotions, not ready to accept the inevitable. There were slogans, internet memes, banners and artwork all over the virtual space and also on the hoardings of his beloved city that he never ditched for greener pastures. Many young directors, actors, critics felt the overwhelming grief of losing their own father, such was the extent of this tragedy. After his death, the coverage he received in the international press was stupefying.

On 15 November 2020, the curtain on Bengal's greatest actor ever came down finally. Satyajit Ray's favourite actor, Sisir Kumar Bhaduri's beloved pupil, the cicerone of three generations of Bengalis—he is the last Renaissance man in the line from Tagore to Ray, ending with him. For a race that battles every day to secure its cultural hegemony and preserve its nuances to pass on to future generations, the vacuum will seem insurmountable.

As long as the spirit of Bengal doesn't die, Soumitra Chatterjee will be remembered for his courage of will and the inner light he shone on others around him.

TEN

A Meandering Quest

In the foreword to her autobiography, Agatha Christie wrote, 'I like living. I have sometimes been wildly despairing, acutely miserable, racked with sorrow, but through it all, I still know quite certainly that just to be alive is a grand thing ... I once saw an old Chinese scroll that I loved. It featured an old man sitting under a tree playing cat's cradle. It was called „Old Man Enjoying the Pleasures of Idleness.‟ I've never forgotten it.'*

All who knew Soumitra Chatterjee will agree that he epitomized the joys of life and living. His reserve of energy had its seeds in an unquenched thirst for life. Looking at him, interacting with him, I, like most others, felt invigorated every time. At the time of writing this book, I reread his essays and plays and found myself standing in front of a rainbow of questions. Why didn't I read them with such attention earlier,

---

* Agatha Christie, *An Autobiography*, Harper Collins, 2010.

I asked myself. Now, the questions remain throbbing quests for me.

As I planned this book, I wanted to find a line of thought which might have lured Soumitra to take up different creative challenges. After his demise, there has been a flurry of writings, magazine issues and a few books which aim to be biographies. Most of them fail for not embracing Soumitra's writings of all forms in their accounts. To me, the relevance of Soumitra's transcendental appeal is in his bid to remain contemporary by confronting the larger questions of his day. To me, even though I followed a linear timeline, the goal is to understand what made Soumitra different from others. Most importantly, seamless transitions between different strands of creative quests make it impossible for him to be compared. Most others fall way short of him in terms of their attempts and achievements.

In this account, hence, I wished to avoid gossips, juicy tales, our fantasies of what we want Soumitra Chatterjee to be. Rather, in my explorations of him in the backdrop of his options and choices, his political stance and his conscious attempts to stay at a distance, I have tried to place him in the context of his time and age. Unless we recall the chronicles of time—his formative years of the '60s and '70s—we will never able to reckon his vision, so distinct from several fellow travellers who had taken rest much earlier than him in the path of life. This account is not a hagiography, nor my memoirs of him, nor like a collection from a host of others fighting to prove their proximity to him.

One of Soumitra's enviable traits was to remain humble and unperturbed by eulogy. He recounted how his father never praised his acting before him. In the same vein, Soumitra mostly felt that the strange silence of Satyajit Ray in accepting his contribution to Ray's cinema was justified. Long back, at a time after *Apur Sansar* was shot but not released, Ray and Soumitra went to watch Sisir Kumar Bhaduri's *Chandragupta*. After the play got over, both went to meet Sisir Kumar in the changing room. Ray mentioned to the thespian that Soumitra had done a good job in the film. Sisir Kumar, without showing a burst of emotion, just quipped, 'Yes, he should.'

Soumitra's eyes lighted up whenever he narrated this incident. Years later, in the late '70s, when one director praised Soumitra's acting in a particular scene in *Devdas*, Uttam Kumar—who had co-acted in the film but was not there in that scene—reacted almost similarly. 'I liked Uttam-da's matter-of-fact response devoid of exaggeration. After acting for so many years, I indeed must be equipped enough to essay these roles with some expertise,' Soumitra reasoned with me in private.

A thoroughly intelligent man, Soumitra's venturing out to different forms of art was, I feel, calculated. There were risks of individual failures, but never a complete debacle. He had a fair perception about his strengths and weaknesses. He never ventured to directing films seriously, he satiated that hunger by directing theatre. He never tried acting in a language unknown to him and his roots. Within his preferred domain, he always pushed boundaries to test his abilities.

In 2003, the last poem of his poetry collection, *Ja Baki Roilo* (What Remains), having the same name as the collection, reads thus:

> *Writing down everything will not be just,*
> *Only the conclusion will be left to be written,*
> *Carrying ritual garments of mourning*
> *Death will come, and wait.*
> *...*
> *Before writing down the whole of it*
> *I wish to hoodwink terror,*
> *Enjoy with the young,*
> *Drawing chariots, waving paper flags,*
> *Then what remains is nothing*
> *But,*
> *Only an insignificant conclusion.**

Asking death to wait in the wings as life was still in full bloom for him. Sixteen years later, through a number of near-terminal illnesses and numbing sorrows, in the last collection of poems, *Bhanga Pother Ranga Dhuloy* (In the Red Dust of the Broken Path), Soumitra concluded the prose-poem as:

> *What is left after this is not to be uttered in a solemn prayer in the house of worship, this time he will strive to be humble, for the sake of that eternally unmarked conclusion.*†

A poet who has accepted his fate, one who has rejoiced in the journey more than the outcome, a life lived fully. Shuttling

---

* Soumitra Chatterjee, *Walking through the Mist*, Tr.: Amitava Nag, Dhauli Books, 2020, pp. 48-49.
† Soumitra Chatterjee, *Bhanga Pother Ranga Dhuloy*, Signet Press, 2019, p. 53—translated by the author.

between creative and performative arts, Soumitra's life had been a longing for an elusive truth about reality. He always maintained that acting should 'resemble life'; his mingling with the commoner to a great extent stemmed from this urge.

In this book, as I meandered over the geography of time, I wished to trace the history of a soul to arrive at an essential portrait. Face to face, not through a glass, dark or pale. Each aspect of Soumitra's creative life as a whole is more than the mere sum of its parts. It is a reflection in the mirror, not a judgement. My aim is to facilitate access to a structured mind to help provide a deeper understanding of Soumitra's lifelong quest for a creative identity. That is why writing this book is excruciatingly difficult and, once done, immensely satisfying for me. I hope it will explore the minds of the readers as well with zeal and ardour.

In front of a painting of young Apu in *Apur Sansar*
(Photo Credit: Sandip Kumar)

In this book, I humbly offer my gratitude to one and all who helped me—with facts, information, pictures, anecdotes. This book is no longer my own. It is by all who helped me arrange the pieces as I looked for congruence.

And, it is Soumitra Chatterjee's. He stayed with me during this journey, hinting to me at possibilities and then leaving me to form my own conclusions. In his minimalism in art and in his sense of life, he will remain a guide, beyond the scope of this book.

Acknowledgements

Aditi Mukherjee
Amal Kundu
Amit Ranjan Biswas
Anindya Banerjee
Arijit Maitra
Arna Seal
Arunaloke Bhattacharyya
Atanu Ghosh
Bilu Dutta
Bodhisattwa Ghosh
Catherine Berge
Chandi Mukherjee
Debasis Mukhopadhyay
Debnath Chattopadhyay
Durba Bandyopadhyay
Joydeep Mukherjee
Jyotirmoy Bhattacharya
Kunal Sen
Meenakshi Chattopadhyay
Mousumi Duttaray
Pinaki De
Piu Mahapatra

Poulami Chatterjee
Purnima Dutta
Raja Mitra
Ranjan Mitra
Roudra Mitra
Sandip Kumar
Sandip Ray
Sanjib Majumdar
Satyaki Ghosh
Shantanu Ray Chaudhuri
Shoma A Chatterji
Shreya Goswami
Shyamal Karmakar
Sohan Banerjee
Soumitra Mitra
Souparna Mitra
Sukumar Roy
Suman Ghosh
Suman Mukherjee
Sumantra Sanyal
Sunit Sengupta
Suranjan Roy

Selected List of Top 150 Films

YEAR	FILM	DIRECTOR
1959	*Apur Sansar*	Satyajit Ray
1960	*Devi*	Satyajit Ray
1960	*Kshudhita Pashan*	Tapan Sinha
1961	*Swaralipi*	Asit Sen
1961	*Teen Kanya (Samapti)*	Satyajit Ray
1961	*Swaymbara*	Asit Sen
1961	*Jhinder Bondi*	Tapan Sinha
1961	*Punascha*	Mrinal Sen
1962	*Shaasti*	Daya Bhai
1962	*Atal Jaler Ahwan*	Ajoy Kar
1962	*Agun*	Asit Sen
1962	*Benarasi*	Arup Guhathakurta
1962	*Abhijan*	Satyajit Ray
1963	*Saat Paake Badha*	Ajoy Kar
1963	*Sesh Prahar*	Prantik
1963	*Barnali*	Ajoy Kar
1964	*Pratinidhi*	Mrinal Sen

YEAR	FILM	DIRECTOR
1964	*Charulata*	Satyajit Ray
1964	*Kinu Goalar Goli*	O C Ganguly
1964	*Ayananta*	Sandhani
1965	*Bakso Badal*	Nityananda Dutta
1965	*Ektuku Basa*	Tarun Majumdar
1965	*Kapurush o Mahapurush (Kapurush)*	Satyajit Ray
1965	*Akash Kusum*	Mrinal Sen
1965	*Ek-e ange eto rup*	Harisadhan Dasgupta
1966	*Monihar*	Salil Sen
1966	*Kanch Kata Hire*	Ajoy Kar
1966	*Joradighir Chaudhuri Paribar*	Ajit Lahiri
1967	*Hathat Dekha*	Nityananda Dutta
1967	*Prastar Saakkhar*	Salil Dutta
1967	*Ajana Sapath*	Salil Sen
1967	*Mahasweta*	Pinaki Mukherjee
1968	*Baghini*	Bijoy Bose
1969	*Teen Bhuvaner Paare*	Ashutosh Bandyopadhyay
1969	*Chena Achena*	Hiren Nag
1969	*Parineeta*	Ajoy Kar
1969	*Aparichito*	Salil Dutta
1970	*Aranyer Din Ratri*	Satyajit Ray
1970	*Pratham Kadam Phool*	Inder Sen
1970	*Padmagolap*	Ajit Lahiri
1970	*Aleyar Alo*	Mangal Chakraborty
1971	*Malyadan*	Ajoy Kar
1971	*Sansar*	Salil Sen
1971	*Khunje Berai*	Salil Dutta

Selected List of Top 150 Films

YEAR	FILM	DIRECTOR
1972	*Aparna*	Salil Sen
1972	*Stree*	Salil Dutta
1973	*Basanta Bilap*	Dinen Gupta
1973	*Natun Diner Alo*	Ajit Lahiri
1973	*Ashani Sanket*	Satyajit Ray
1973	*Bilet Ferot (Rakta)*	Chidananda Dasgupta
1973	*Sesh Pristhay Dekhun*	Salil Dutta
1974	*Jadi Jantem*	Jatrik
1974	*Sonar Kella*	Satyajit Ray
1974	*Asati*	Salil Dutta
1975	*Chutir Phande*	Salil Sen
1975	*Sansar Simante*	Tarun Majumdar
1975	*Nishimrigaya*	Dinen Gupta
1976	*Nandita*	Swadesh Sarkar
1976	*Datta*	Ajoy Kar
1976	*Sudur Niharika*	Sushil Mukherjee
1977	*Babumoshai*	Salil Dutta
1977	*Mantramugdha*	Arabinda Mukhopadhyay
1977	*Pratima*	Palash Bandopadhyay
1978	*Pranay Pasha*	Mangal Chakraborty
1979	*Joi Baba Felunath*	Satyajit Ray
1979	*Devdas*	Dilip Roy
1979	*Ganadevata*	Tarun Majumdar
1979	*Naukadubi*	Ajoy Kar
1979	*Job Charnocker Bibi*	Jayanta Bhattacharya
1980	*Pankhiraj*	Pijush Basu
1980	*Hirak Rajar Deshe*	Satyajit Ray
1980	*Darpachurna*	Dilip Roy

YEAR	FILM	DIRECTOR
1981	Father	Dilip Mukherjee
1981	Pratisodh	Sukhen Das
1982	Rasamayir Rasikota	Amal Sur
1982	Bijoyini	Palash Bandopadhyay
1982	Matir Swarga	Bijoy Bose
1982	Preyashi	Srikanta Guhathakurata
1983	Chena Achena	Pinaki Chaudhuri
1983	Agradani	Palash Bandopadhyay
1983	Indira	Dinen Gupta
1984	Amargeeti	Tarun Majumdar
1984	Simanto Raag	Pradip Bhattacharjee
1985	Ghare Baire	Satyajit Ray
1985	Sandhya Pradeep	Anjan Mukherjee
1985	Baikunther Will	Sushil Mukherjee
1986	Kony	Saroj De
1986	Shyam Saheb	Salil Dutta
1986	Basundhara	Shekhar Chattopadhyay
1986	Atanka	Tapan Sinha
1988	Agni Sanket	Arup Dutta
1988	The Bengali Night	Nicolas Klotz
1990	Ganashatru	Satyajit Ray
1990	Ekti Jiban	Raja Mitra
1991	Mahaprithivi	Mrinal Sen
1991	Path o Prasad	Tarun Majumdar
1992	Antardhan	Tapan Sinha
1992	Shakha Proshakha	Satyajit Ray
1993	Pashanda Pandit	Shibaprasad Sen
1994	Uttaran	Sandip Ray

Selected List of Top 150 Films

YEAR	FILM	DIRECTOR
1994	*Wheel Chair*	Tapan Sinha
1995	*Kakababu Here Gelen*	Pinaki Chaudhuri
1996	*Sopan*	Ajay Banerjee
1996	*Vrindaban Film Studio*	Lamberto Lambertini
1996	*Lathi*	Prabhat Roy
1997	*Nayantara*	Raja Mitra
1998	*Ajab Gayer Ajab Katha*	Tapan Sinha
1999	*Atmiya Swajan*	Raja Sen
1999	*Asukh*	Rituparno Ghosh
2000	*Paramaitar Ekdin*	Aparna Sen
2001	*Dekha*	Goutam Ghose
2002	*Sanjhbatir Rupkatha*	Anjan Das
2003	*Abaar Aranye*	Goutam Ghose
2003	*Bhalo Theko*	Gautam Haldar
2003	*Hemanter Pakhi*	Urmi Chakraborty
2003	*Patalghar*	Avijit Chowdhury
2004	*Shadows of Time*	Florian Gallenberger
2004	*Debipaksha*	Raja Sen
2005	*Nishijapon*	Sandip Ray
2005	*Krantikal*	Shekhar Das
2005	*15 Park Avenue*	Aparna Sen
2006	*Padakkhep*	Suman Ghosh
2007	*Ballynggunge Court*	Pinaki Chaudhuri
2009	*Angshumaner Chhobi*	Atanu Ghosh
2009	*Dwando*	Suman Ghosh
2009	*Kalbela*	Goutam Ghose
2010	*Ami Aadu*	Somnath Gupta
2011	*Nobel Chor*	Suman Ghosh

YEAR	FILM	DIRECTOR
2012	*Aparajita Tumi*	Aniruddha Roy Chowdhury
2012	*Paanch Adhyay*	Pratim D Gupta
2013	*Maach Mishti & More*	Mainak Bhaumik
2013	*Shunyo Awnko*	Goutam Ghose
2013	*Alik Sukh*	Nandita Roy and Shiboprosad Mukherjee
2013	*Rupkatha Noy*	Atanu Ghosh
2014	*Punascha*	Souvik Mitra
2015	*Belaseshe*	Nandita Roy and Shiboprosad Mukherjee
2015	*Ahalya (Short)*	Sujoy Ghosh
2015	*Selfie*	Sovon Tarafder
2016	*Peace Haven*	Suman Ghosh
2016	*Praktan*	Nandita Roy and Shiboprosad Mukherjee
2016	*Bridge*	Amit Ranjan Biswas
2017	*Posto*	Nandita Roy and Shiboprosad Mukherjee
2017	*Mayurakshi*	Atanu Ghosh
2018	*Basu Paribar*	Suman Ghosh
2018	*Kusumitar Gappo*	Hrishikesh Mandal
2018	*Manojder Adbhut Bari*	Anindya Chatterjee
2018	*Shonar Pahar*	Parambrata Chatterjee
2019	*Sanjhbati*	Leena Ganguly and Saibal Banerjee
2020	*Barun Babur Bandhu*	Anik Dutta
2022	*Abhijan*	Parambrata Chatterjee
2022	*Belashuru*	Nandita Roy and Shiboprosad Mukherjee

List of Plays

YEAR	NAME OF PLAY	INVOLVED AS
1957	*Prafulla*	Actor (Dir: Sisir Kumar Bhaduri)
1963	*Tapasi*	Actor (Dir: Debnarayan Gupta)
1968	*Sesh Rakshya*	Actor (Dir: Anup Kumar)
1971	*Andhayug*	Actor (Dir: Ajitesh Bandyopadhyay)
1971	*Bidhi o Byatikram*	Director, Playwright
1972	*Bidehi*	Actor, Director, Playwright
1972	*Sree Hari Sahay*	Director
1973	*Crushbiddho Cuba*	Actor (Dir: Utpal Dutt)
1973, 1983	*Rajkumar*	Actor, Director, Playwright
1974	*Chhoto Bakulpurer Jatri*	Director
1974	*Himalaye Jibanta Manush*	Director
1976	*20se June*	Actor (Dir: Jnanesh Mukherjee)

YEAR	NAME OF PLAY	INVOLVED AS
1978, 1986	*Namjiban*	Actor, Director, Playwright (with Deepa Chatterjee)
1984	*Ratnadeep*	Actor, Director
1987	*Phera*	Actor, Director, Playwright
1988, 2000	*Neelkantha*	Actor, Director, Playwright
1990	*Ghatak Biday*	Actor, Director, Playwright
1992	*Darpane Sarat Sashi*	Actor, Director
1994	*Chandanpurer Chor*	Actor, Director, Playwright
1995	*Tiktiki*	Actor, Director, Playwright
1995	*Pratikshya*	Actor (Dir: Kaushik Sen)
1996	*Nyaymurti*	Actor, Director, Playwright
1997	*Bilwamangal*	Actor, Director
1998	*Pran Tapasya*	Actor, Director, Playwright
2002	*Aar Ekti Din*	Actor, Director, Playwright
2003	*Kurbani*	Actor, Director, Playwright
2004	*Arohan*	Actor, Director, Playwright
2006	*Homapakhi*	Actor, Director
2008	*Atmakatha*	Actor, Director, Playwright
2010	*Raja Lear*	Actor (Dir: Suman Mukhopadhyay)
2010	*Tritiyo Anka Otoeb*	Actor, Director, Playwright
2012	*Chhariganga*	Actor, Director, Playwright
2013	*Sabjanta*	Director, Playwright
2014	*Kalmrigaya*	Actor (Dir: Poulami Bose)
2014	*Phera*	Actor (Dir: Poulami Bose)
2016	*Boshtomi*	Actor, Director, Playwright
2018	*Ghatak Biday*	Actor (Dir: Poulami Bose)

Selected Works in Doordarshan

TYPE	NAME	DIRECTOR
Play	*Malancha*	Shyamal Sen
Play	*Mahasindhur Opar Hote*	Soumitra Chatterjee
Telefilm	*Stree Ka Patra*	Soumitra Chatterjee (didn't act)
Telefilm	*Chandrabati Katha*	Swapan Saha
Telefilm	*Upalabdhi*	Susanta Pal Chaudhuri
Telefilm	*Gokul*	Arundhati Devi
Telefilm	*Nirupama*	Bijay Chatterjee
Telefilm	*Dadaji*	Bijay Chatterjee
Telefilm	*Jyotishi*	Dipankar De
Telefilm	*Sambhabi*	Sudipto Chatterjee
Tele Serial	*Utsaber Rat*	Bibhas Chakraborty
Tele Serial	*Payomukh*	Manas Bhowmik
Tele Serial	*Dena Paona*	Bijay Chatterjee
Tele Serial	*Debatar Byadhi*	Raja Sen
Tele Serial	*Solution X*	Jagannath Guha
Tele Serial	*Ghurghutiyar Kando*	Bibhas Chakraborty

TYPE	NAME	DIRECTOR
Tele Serial	*Golokdham Rahasya*	Bibhas Chakraborty
Tele Serial	*Arogya Niketan*	Raja Sen
Tele Serial	*Ichchhapuran*	Ramaprasad Banik

Bibliography

Alok Chattopadhyay & Manas Chakraborty (Eds.), *Soumitra*, Sristi Prakasani (second edition from Prativas), 2000.

Amitava Nag, *Beyond Apu: 20 Favourite Film Roles of Soumitra Chatterjee*, HarperCollins Publishers, 2016.

Amitava Nag, *Murmurs: Silent Steals with Soumitra Chatterjee*, Blue Pencil Publishers, 2021.

Anasua Roy Choudhury, *Aaj Kaal Porshur Prante*, a long interview, Krantik (second edition from Prativas), 2000.

Aniruddha Dhar, *Sera ponchisti Soumitra nirman*, Prativas, 2019.

Arjun Sengupta & Partha Mukherjee, *Soumitra Chatterjee: A Life in Cinema, Theatre, Poetry & Painting*, Niyogi Books, 2021.

Arunendra Mukherjee, *Naam Soumitra*, Arkadeep, 1995.

Chandan Goswami (Ed.), *Soumitra Chattopadhyayer Charitrer Michhile 58 bochhor*, Dey's Publishing, 2016.

Jibendu Ray (Ed.), *Soumitra Chattopadhyay*, Alok Asar, 1992.

Jyotirmoy Bhattacharya (Ed.), *Forms Within* (collection of paintings and essays published during Soumitra Chatterjee's maiden painting exhibition titled 'Forms Within'), Art Alinda, 2013.

Mohd. Jahangir & Anwar Hossain Pintu (Eds.), *Soumitra Chattopadhyay*, Mawla Brothers, Dhaka, 2002.

Shailendra Haldar (Ed.), *Bishay Soumitra* (A collection of poems/limericks on the occasion of Soumitra's sixtieth birthday by noted Bengali poets), Ashirwad Prakashan, 1994.

Soumitra Chatterjee & Asrukumar Sikder (Eds.) *Selected Ekshan—Vol. II*, Saptarshi Prakashan, 2011.

Soumitra Chatterjee & Asrukumar Sikder (Eds.), *Selected Ekshan—Vol. I*, Saptarshi Prakashan, 2009.

Soumitra Chatterjee & Nirmalya Acharya (Eds.), *Amaar Katha—autobiography of Binodini Dasi*, Subarnarekha, 1964.

Soumitra Chatterjee & Nirmalya Acharya (Eds.), *Amaar Katha o Ananya rachana—autobiography of Binodini Dasi*, Subarnarekha, 1969.

Soumitra Chatterjee, *Aarohan* (play), Aajkal Publishers Ltd., 1994.

Soumitra Chatterjee, *Agrapathikera* (book of essays), Aajkal Publishers Ltd., 2010.

Soumitra Chatterjee, *Antameel* (book of poems), Signet Press, 2019.

Soumitra Chatterjee, *Atmaparichay* (book of essays), Patrabharati, 2020.

Soumitra Chatterjee, *Bhanga pather ranga dhulay* (book of poems), Signet Press, 2018.

Soumitra Chatterjee, *Byaktigoto nakshatramala* (book of poems), Biswabani Publication, 1976.

Soumitra Chatterjee, *Charitrer Sandhane* (book of essays), Saptarshi, 2006.

Soumitra Chatterjee, *Chhora sangraha* (collection of selected limericks), Bhraman Bichitra, 1999.

Soumitra Chatterjee, *Dharabahik tomar jole* (book of poems), Sristi Prakashan, 2001.

Soumitra Chatterjee, *Drashta* (translation of Khalil Gibran's 'The Prophet'), Aajkal Publishers Ltd., 1998.

Soumitra Chatterjee, *Ekshan* (magazine edited with Nirmalya Acharya from 1961 to 1979).

Soumitra Chatterjee, *Gadya Sangraha—Vol. I & Vol. II* (2 volumes of essays edited by Ranjan Mitra and Shamik Banerjee), Dey's Publishing, 2016.

Soumitra Chatterjee, *Galpaguchchho Natyarupe* (collection of Tagore's stories as plays), Thema, 2015.

Soumitra Chatterjee, *Granthi* (book of essays), Aajkal Publishers Ltd., 1994.

Soumitra Chatterjee, *Hay chirojol* (book of poems), Dey's Publishing, 1992.

Soumitra Chatterjee, *Hey sayankal* (book of poems), Dey's Publishing, 1995.

Soumitra Chatterjee, *Holud roduur* (book of poems), Barnaparichay Publishers Pvt. Ltd., 2010.

Bibliography

Soumitra Chatterjee, *Ja baki roilo* (book of poems), Sasadhar Prakashani, 2003.

Soumitra Chatterjee, *Jalapropater dhare danrabo bole* (book of poems), Annapurna Publishing, 1975.

Soumitra Chatterjee, *Janma jaay janma jaabe* (book of poems), Dey's Publishing, 1998.

Soumitra Chatterjee, *Kabita Samagra* (anthology of poetry), Signet Press, 2014.

Soumitra Chatterjee, *Kaleidoscope* (book of poems), Signet Press, 2015.

Soumitra Chatterjee, *Madhyarater Sanket* (book of poems), Signet Press. 2012.

Soumitra Chatterjee, *Manik-dar Sange* (memoir on Satyajit Ray), Aajkal Publishers Ltd., 1993.

Soumitra Chatterjee, *Nati-natnir chhora* (book of limericks), Ray Mangal, 1998.

Soumitra Chatterjee, *Natya Samagra Vol. I, Vol. II & Vol. III* (3 volumes of plays), Ananda Publishers, 2015.

Soumitra Chatterjee, *Padmabeej-er mala* (book of poems), Aajkal Publishers Ltd., 1995.

Soumitra Chatterjee, *Parichay* (book of essays), Prakash Bhawan, 2013.

Soumitra Chatterjee, *Pore aache chandaner chita* (book of poems), Biswabani Publication, 1983.

Soumitra Chatterjee, *Prantapasya* (play), Aajkal Publishers Ltd., 1999.

Soumitra Chatterjee, *Pratidin tobo gatha* (audio play), Aajkal Publishers Ltd., 2009.

Soumitra Chatterjee, *Rajkumar* (play), Subarnarekha, 1975.

Soumitra Chatterjee, *Sabdara amar bagane* (book of poems), Biswabani Publication, 1981.

Soumitra Chatterjee, *Sisir Kumar* (collected essays on Sisir Kumar Bhaduri), Aajkal Publishers Ltd., 2013.

Soumitra Chatterjee, *Soumitra Chattopadhyay Nirbachito Prabandha Sangroho* (book of selected essays), Natyachinta foundation, 2006.

Soumitra Chatterjee, *Soumitra Chattopadhyay-er srestho kabita* (selected collection of poems), Dey's Publishing, 1993.

Soumitra Chatterjee, *Swagoto* (book of essays), Fourth Estate Publication, 1996.

Soumitra Chatterjee, *Swechchhabandi ashar kuhoke* (book of poems), Signet Press, 2018.

Soumitra Chatterjee, *The Master and I* ('Manik-dar Sange' translated by Arunava Sinha), Supernova Publishers, 2014.

Soumitra Chatterjee, *Tiktiki* (play), Aajkal Publishers Ltd., 1997.

Soumitra Chatterjee, *Tin Ekanka* (book of plays), Aajkal Publishers Ltd., 2004.

Soumitra Chatterjee, *Walking through the mist* (selected poems translated by Amitava Nag), Dhauli Books, 2020.

Soumitra Mitra (Ed.), *Soumitra Chattoadhyay: Dekhi Bismaye*, Purba Paschim, Dey's Publishing, 2021.

Major Awards

YEAR	AWARD
1995	Filmfare Lifetime Achievement Award
1997	Ujala Anandalok Lifetime Achievement Award
1999	Sangeet Natak Academy from the Government of India
1999	International film festival, Napoli, Italy—Lifetime Achievement Award
2000	'Officier des Arts et Metiers' awarded by the French Government
2004	Padmabhushan, Government of India
2007	Best Actor for Padakkhep at National Film Awards
2007	BFJA Lifetime Achievement Award
2009	E-TV Sera Bangali, 24 Ghanta Sera Bangali, Star Ananda Lifetime Achievement Award
2012	Dadashaheb Phalke Award, Government of India
2012	Lifetime Achievement award by West Bengal government for contribution to Bengali cinema on the occasion of Uttam Kumar's 32nd Death anniversary
2016	Kazi Sabyasachi Memorial Award by the Government of Bangladesh
2017	Banga Bibhushan, Government of West Bengal, India
2017	ABP Ananda Sera-r Sera
2018	The Legion of Honour' awarded by the French Government

Besides these, Soumitra Chatterjee won more than 10 Best Actor awards at several award ceremonies including international ones.

Soumitra Chatterjee had been conferred honorary DLitt from the following universities:

- Rabindra Bharati University, Burdwan University,
- Vidyasagar University, Kalyani University,
- Deshikottam from Vishva Bharati University,
- Bengal Engineering and Science University,
- Jadavpur University, Assam University, Presidency University.

Special Thanks to Mr Ranjan Mitra, editor, for validating the filmography and other necessary details.

ALSO IN SPEAKING TIGER

ENTER STAGE RIGHT
The Alkazi/Padamsee Family Memoir
Feisal Alkazi

Bombay, 1943. The young Parsi actress who was playing Salome in the newly founded Theatre Group's production of Oscar Wilde's eponymously titled play drew the line at performing the *Dance of the Seven Veils*, a sort of 'Biblical striptease'. So director Sultan Padamsee's 19-year-old sister Roshen stepped in. And met the handsome, intense Arab who played the male lead—Ebrahim Alkazi. In 1946, they were married.

Thus was forged one of the greatest alliances in the world of theatre and art in post-Independence India. Ebrahim Alkazi took English theatre from its early beginnings in Bombay to national and even international acclaim as he directed and acted in more than a hundred plays, ranging from *Oedipus Rex*, *Murder in the Cathedral* and *Macbeth* in the 1950s, to *Ashadh Ka Ek Din*, *Andha Yug* and *Tughlaq* in the '60s and '70s. As director of the fabled National School of Drama from 1962 to 1977, he launched some of the finest actors of our times, including Om Shivpuri, Om Puri, Naseeruddin Shah, Rohini Hattangadi, Manohar Singh and Uttara Baokar. Chief costume designer and seamstress for all his productions was Roshen Alkazi.

In 1977, when Ebrahim and Roshen decided to open Art Heritage in Delhi, it gave a new dimension to the world of art, as the leading artists of the day, including M.F. Husain, Krishen Khanna, F.N. Souza, Tyeb Mehta, K.G. Subramanyam and Laxma Goud, flocked to this space that was not just a 'commercial' gallery, but a foundation for documenting and preserving the arts.

With more than 50 rare photographs, *Enter Stage Right* is the story of theatre in India as it has never been told before...to be treasured by theatre buffs, and savoured by anyone who loves a good story.

ALSO IN SPEAKING TIGER

ZOHRA!
A Biography in Four Acts
Ritu Menon

Zohra Segal (1912-2014) spanned an Indian century of the arts and became the only woman to make a mark in all the performing arts, with the exception of music, within the country and abroad. This elegant biography traces her remarkable journey.

Born into a family with connections to the nawabs of Rampur, Zohra Mumtazullah Khan chose adventure over tradition when she was eighteen, travelling to Germany to learn modern dance. For the rest of her life, she continued to defy convention and was associated with transformative initiatives in the arts. In 1935, she was recruited by the bohemian genius Uday Shankar and toured the world with his dance troupe, until he disbanded it. In 1943, she set up a unique dance school in Lahore with her husband Kameshwar Segal, eight years her junior. In Bombay two years later, she joined Prithvi Theatres, founded by the legendary Prithviraj Kapoor. For the next fourteen years she travelled across India, taking socially relevant plays directly to the people—through the turbulence of Partition and the heady idealism following Independence, and the tragedy of Kameshwar's suicide.

In 1962, Zohra went to London on a drama scholarship and stayed on for twentyfive years, becoming part of a tiny band of Asian artistes who would change the complexion of British theatre and television through pioneering TV series and films like *Doctor Who*, *Jewel in the Crown* and *Bhaji on the Beach*. Back in India, she was surprised to find Bollywood at her door when she was well past eighty. Playing the unconventional grandmother—by turns charming and crusty—she became a household name.

In this biography of the unlikely star, Ritu Menon helps us understand both the performer and the person, and the exciting times she lived in.